The
Best Little
INSTRUCTION
Book Ever!
POCKET EDITION

© 2010 Time Inc. Home Entertainment
Published by Time Inc. Home Entertainment

Time Inc.
1271 Avenue of the Americas
New York, New York 10020

ISBN 10: 1-60320-854-2
ISBN 13: 978-1-60320-854-3
Library of Congress Control Number: 2009940853

Printed in Mexico.

We welcome your comments and suggestions about
Time Inc. Home Entertainment Books.
Please write to us at:
Time Inc. Home Entertainment Books
Attention: Book Editors
PO Box 11016
Des Moines, IA 50336-1016

If you would like to order any of our hardcover
Collector's Edition books, please call us at
1-800-327-6388.
(Monday through Friday, 7:00 a.m.— 8:00 p.m. or
Saturday, 7:00 a.m.— 6:00 p.m. Central Time).

GOLF®
MAGAZINE

The Best Little INSTRUCTION Book Ever!

From the Top 100 Teachers in America

EDITED BY DAVID DENUNZIO

GOLF
MAGAZINE
TOP
100
TEACHERS
IN AMERICA

POCKET EDITION

Time Inc.
HOME ENTERTAINMENT

Your Best Golf Ever!

espite any success you've had in the past, the book in your hands is going to help you shoot lower scores and better enjoy your golfing experience. Confident claims no doubt, but they're easily made considering the source of the more than 1,000 tips, drills and lessons contained within. Each one comes straight out of the pages of *GOLF Magazine*, the most widely read golf publication in the world. With a near-50 year legacy of award-winning instruction, *GOLF* has become the leader in the way the game is taught and played. Moreover, our instruction is driven by the single greatest collection of teaching experts in the game: the Top 100 Teachers. Members of this elite group are chosen not only for their swing knowledge and experience, but also for their teaching skills and knack for developing methods that make

the game easier to learn. Some of the Top 100 Teachers you know by name—the ones that work with the major stars on the professional tours. Others are teaching legends with hall-of-fame status. But all of them are dedicated to helping golfers just like you get better and making sure these changes stick.

Since its inception in 1996, the Top 100 Teachers have produced more than 3,500 pages of instruction in *GOLF Magazine*. This book represents their greatest hits, so to speak, organized to build your game from the ground up the right way and, better yet, make it last for a lifetime. Use their advice to hit the ball farther, putt better, chip closer and beat anything the course throws at you. With the help of the Top 100 Teachers, your best golf ever is just around the corner

DAVID DENUNZIO,
INSTRUCTION EDITOR, GOLF MAGAZINE.

What's Inside

Better swings—and scores—are a page turn away, courtesy of the Top 100 Teachers in America.

CONTENTS

What you do before your rounds and the time spent between them determines the scores you shoot and how quickly you can lower them.

The fact that you're holding this book in your hands means you're serious about your game and about improving. The majority of these pages are dedicated to helping you get around the course in as few strokes as possible. This section, however, focuses on what you need to do between rounds to make sure the lessons stick. With the help of the Top 100 Teachers, you'll learn how to warm up before play to get off to good starts, how to make your practice time serious learning time, how to select the gear that will help you save strokes and how to make your lessons more effective. Armed with this knowledge, you'll optimize the non-playing part of your game—a period that's vastly larger than the hours you actually spend on the course—so you can put your swing on autopilot and shoot the scores you want.

1

1

PREPARING TO PLAY

How to get your round motoring out of the
blocks even before you hit your first shot

The Right Way to Loosen Up for Play

"I need a quick and easy way to warm up my swing—I'm always late to my tee time."

"Follow these quick steps for peak performance every time you tee it up."

DAVE PHILLIPS
Titleist Performance Institute
Oceanside, Calif.

FUNDAMENTAL

DO THIS!
Whether your pre-round warm-up time is an hour (ideal) or 15 minutes (typical), you have time to get ready for one of your best rounds.

STEP 1
Walk briskly to the driving range to get your blood moving, then warm up. Hold two clubs together and swing them in circles, doing 10 reps with each arm. This prepares your shoulders for demands of the golf swing.

STEP 2
Rest the clubs on the ground and hold them vertically, securing your hands on top of the grips *[right]*. Keep your hands there and do 10 squats to warm up your knees, calves and hips.

NOTE
Even if you don't hit another ball after the last step, your body will be primed to hit a good drive on the first tee and sustain a high level of performance throughout your round.

TRY THIS!

START WITH YOUR SHORT GAME SHOTS

Statistics show golfers score better on the middle 10 holes than the first and last four. It's easy to see how the pressure to shoot a certain score might make you nervous and result in poor scores at the finish. But poor play on the first four holes? Perhaps this is because you're not prepared to scramble when you miss the first few greens. This emphasizes the importance of warming up your short-game feel and touch—chips, pitches and putts— before heading to the first tee. A complete-game warm-up is optimal, but when you're short on time, warm up your scoring game first!
—*Top 100 Teacher Dave Pelz*

STEP 3

Hit your short irons for a solid 10 minutes. Start with slow, three-quarter length swings and gradually build to full swings. After 10 minutes of hitting balls you can stretch your arm, leg and core muscles however you like without risking a visit to the chiropractor the next day.

2 | How to Hit Practice Balls

"I go to the range, but don't follow a set routine, and I think it's making my time useless."

"There's a right way to practice to improve skills and rhythm—and you look cool doing it!"

JOHN ELLIOTT, JR.
Golden Ocala Golf and
Equestrian Club
Ocala, Fla.

THE PROBLEM
You go through a bucket of range balls like a wave of locusts through a cornfield.

THE SOLUTION
When you beat balls at a machine-gun pace you're not helping your game much. You need to set up to the ball correctly every time, and also take the time to follow through completely, study your ball flight and landing patterns, and then decompress and get ready for the next shot. In other words, you need to practice like you play.

HOW TO DO IT
Watch Tour players on the driving range. Most pros follow a six-step procedure that takes them from ball to ball in a deliberate, measured way that mimics how they approach each shot on the golf course. If you mimic that procedure, you're guaranteed to become a better ball striker.

STEP 1
Tip over a bucket of balls and, with your club in your right hand, pull a ball out of the pile and drag it over to a spot where you can hit it.

STEP 4
Make a complete, balanced swing so that you're facing the target and most of your weight is on your left foot. Study the flight of your ball, and stay in this position until it has landed.

STEP 2

Stand behind your ball and pick your target. Step into address—first with your right foot and then with your left—while glancing at your target.

STEP 3

Once you're comfortable in your address position and have visualized your target line, waggle the club once or twice to loosen your wrists, and then swing away.

STEP 5

As the ball comes to a stop, remove your right hand from the grip and allow the club to slide down the fingers of your left hand until it feels light and balanced in your hand.

STEP 6

Now "present" the handle of the club to your right hand, release your left hand, and go back to Step 1. Now you're practicing like a pro!

DRILL

TRY THIS!

THREE WAYS TO MAKE PRACTICE TIME SERIOUS LEARNING TIME

1: Practice with the club that allows you to hit the fairway consistently, even if it's a 3-wood. Your driver isn't the only club you can hit from the tee box.

2: Hit punch shots with your 7-iron to ingrain the feel of solid impact. Don't try to kill the ball when attempting these. Use a three-quarter swing and focus on striking the ball with your hands ahead of the clubhead at contact.

3: Hit shots with the sole purpose of maintaining your posture from start to finish. You'll be amazed by how much good balance affects your swing.
—*Top 100 Teacher Rod Lidenberg*

"I'd save serious strokes if I could ony hole a few more putts. What's the secret?"

"Try these six tips for making your time on the practice putting green pay off."

GALE PETERSON
Sea Island
Golf Learning Center
St. Simons Island, Ga.

1: SAVE TRICK SHOTS FOR POOL

It might be fun to slide a 60-foot putt through a slalom course of tees, but on the course you're more likely to miss the straight 3-footers.

2: PLAY FOR KEEPS

Have a nine-hole putting contest with a buddy. This is the best way to prepare for a match. You'll be forced to make putts under competitive pressure, just as you will on the course.

3: NEVER GIVE AN INCH

Ever laugh at a guy practicing 1-foot putts and then lose to him? Practice some short ones. You'll win more matches by assuming you'll never be conceded a putt.

4: DON'T BE A DRONE

Don't repeatedly drain the same well-trodden putt, as if every one you face will be a 6-footer with the same break. Practice putts that vary in length and slope to more accurately match the putts in a typical round.

5: TALK IS CHEAP

Don't look at the practice green only as a place to unload a new batch of jokes. If you take putting practice seriously, your results will speak for themselves.

6: SET GOALS

Try to make 10 3-footers in a row along a tee- or coin-marked wheel around the cup. If you miss on No. 9, start over. Then try three in a row from 10 feet. Goal-setting breeds discipline and confidence.

"I fear hitting my opening tee shot. How can I remove my first-tee jitters?"

"Whether you warm up or not, follow these steps to make sure you're first shot is a good one."

BRIAN MOGG
Golden Bear Golf Club at
Keene's Pointe
Windermere, Fla.

FUNDAMENTAL

DO THIS!
Run through this five-item checklist before you step up to hit your first tee shot. It won't take long, and it can go a long way toward making that first drive a good one.

COUNT YOUR CLUBS
You're only allowed 14 sticks in your bag, and while your buddies might not call a penalty on you, an official certainly will if you ever play in a formal event. Plus, you want to make sure you didn't leave your trusty 7-iron in the backyard.

GEAR UP
Run through the pockets in your bag. Some necessities you'll need for every round are a glove, plenty of tees, a pencil, coins or markers and your scorecard. During the summer, make sure you're armed with sunblock and lip balm.

TAKE A BREAK

Lag behind your group as you walk to the first tee, close your eyes and think about the day ahead. Devise a game plan not only for your swing, but for how you'll conduct yourself during your round. Without this kind of mental strategy, you won't find your groove until it's much too late.

TARGET YOUR FOCUS

Picture landing the ball in a bull's-eye and erase any negative thoughts. Your first tee shot is important: The positive emotions that come with getting off to a good start can send your energy and focus to the level you need to play your best.

CHECK YOUR SWING

Swing to the top of your backswing, stop, and look over your right shoulder to check your position. You may notice that the club is laid off, or that the clubface is wide open. You'll want to know about these things before you tee off so you won't have to search for clues or experiment with dangerous swing changes.

5 | How to Get More from Your Lessons

"I don't feel like I'm getting my true money's worth from my pro. Is it me, or him?"

"Learning is a two-way street. Here's how to make sure it's pointing toward improvement."

RICK MCCORD
McCord Golf Academy at
Orange Lake CC
Orlando, Fla.

STRATEGY

1: CHOOSE YOUR CLASSROOM

If you're looking to improve your swing and ball striking, the range is the best place. But if you want better course management, take a playing lesson.

2: SET EXPECTATIONS

Before the lesson, tell your instructor what you're looking to improve and how much you'd like to accomplish. Don't expect to drop 10 strokes after one lesson.

3: FIND THE RIGHT PRO

Ask your pals for suggestions—or find one of our Top 100 teachers at golf.com. Call the pros and interview them. Ask them about their teaching style—what you can expect—then pick a teacher who appeals to your needs.

The student-teacher relationship is key—you need an instructor you can trust.

4: HIT REWIND

Start every practice session with a review of what you've been taught. Start with the basics then go through your last lesson. Don't abandon the teachings if you're not getting perfect results—keep at it and you'll start to see the payoff.

5: COOL DOWN

Spend another 15 minutes on the range after your lesson. Work on your own to relax and apply what you've just learned from your teacher. Also, take notes, and if your pro tapes the lesson, taking home a video is even better.

6: DON'T RUSH

Whether you're coming from home or the office, don't blaze into the parking lot and quickly throw on your spikes. To get your mind and body in optimal condition, arrive at your lesson 15 minutes early to loosen up.

How to Get the Right Gear

"Should I improve my game before buying new clubs? I'd feel like I'd be wasting money."

"Even if your swing is sound, it won't do you much good if you're playing the wrong gear."

JIM HARDY
Jim Hardy Golf
Houston, Tex.
2007 Teacher of the Year

FUNDAMENTAL

FLY SOLO
Go alone and let the salesman help you make decisions. Many golfers end up making bad purchases based on advice from a buddy that knows very little about equipment.

CAP YOUR WALLET
Follow a budget to prevent buyer's remorse. Set a price range for the final bill rather than for each individual item. This will give you the flexibility to spend more money on one thing and less on another.

STEP IN IT
When you're buying gear, dont' forget about your feet. Shoes have become an important piece of the gear puzzle. Make sure a shoe is comfortable right out of the box. It's not going to fit any better on the course. Also look for a lighter athletic or sneaker-type shoe if you prefer to walk over riding in a cart.

Smart golf begins with smart equipment-buying decisions.

IRON OUT YOUR BAG

The average golfer needs more hybrids and fewer long irons. Once the salesman knows what type of courses you play, he can tell you what ratio of irons to wedges to hybrids you need.

GET FIT

A fitting for woods, irons, a driver, grip size and balls takes at most 30 minutes. Most stores have a launch monitor or a simulator so the salesman can fit you and then recommend clubs for your game. A short stint with a clubfitter can possibly give you 20 extra yards off the tee.

TELL THE TRUTH

If you decide to go the fitting route, be honest about how you hit the ball, how you strategize and what clubs you favor. Telling the truth about your game is the only way to get a proper fit.

"Look for clubs with lofts that fill the gaps in your set, whether they're between your longest iron and your most lofted wood, or between your wedges."

—Jim Hardy

1

Elite golfers base their swings on the principle that good positions lead to better positions in the segments of the swing that follow.

The swing is a complex beast. This statement is no surprise to anyone who has tried to build one. Those that excel at it are the ones who commit to constant practice and study to turn the complexities into simple, repeatable actions. Unfortunately, you can't simply learn a swing and expect it to take your game where you want it to go. You must understand it.

Like most instruction books, this one starts with your address. But unlike the rest this one breaks down every facet of the swing that follows and provides insights and checkpoints you can use to improve every inch of your motion. It's a simple approach because correcting even a few positions—or learning how to get into them correctly for the first time—automatically improves the positions that follow.

2

UNDERSTANDING YOUR SWING

How to make it simple and repeatable
for consistent success

"I never think about my grip. Is this something I should be practicing?"

"A solid grip allows you to make a natural motion and stops errors in their tracks. Here's how to get one."

BRIAN MOGG
Golden Bear Golf Club at Keene's Pointe
Windermere, Fla.

STEP 1
Do this without a glove to really get the feel of how to grip your clubs properly. Hold the handle against your outstretched left hand. The grip should extend diagonally from the fatty portion of your hand (just below your pinkie) to the middle crease of your index finger.

STEP 2 ➡
Put your glove on and place the club how you had it in Step 1. Then, curl your fingers around the handle so that the fatty portion of your hand is on top. You should apply pressure with the last three fingers of your left hand. (You shouldn't feel any pressure in your palm.)

STEP 3 →

When you position your right hand, the handle should rest across the base of your right pinkie to the top crease in your index finger. This ensures that you grip the club with your fingers, not your palm. Wrap your fingers around the underside of the grip and place the fatty portion of your right hand on top of your left thumb.

STEP 4 →

Hold your grip out in front of you and check that the Vs formed by your thumbs and forefingers point to the right side of your face. Depending on your preference, rest your right pinkie in the crease between your left index and middle fingers (overlapping grip) or wedge it between them (interlocking).

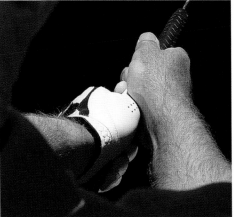

FIND THE PERFECT AMOUNT OF SQUEEZE

I hear it all the time: "Should I grip the club lightly or firmly?" I recommend that you grip the club as though you were gluing your hands to it. You want complete contact. Every bit of the insides of your fingers should be touching the handle—no gaps, no air pockets and no spaces.

Next, hold your club over your right shoulder and pretend you're about to throw it end over end without actually letting go of the club. The feeling you have when holding your club and going through the throwing motion is a good fit for your grip and grip pressure."

—*Top 100 Teacher Bob Toski*

"What's better: a weak grip or a strong grip? Mine changes on every swing."

"It's up to you. What's more critical is that your hands work together, not as independent parts."

JASON CARBONE
Jim McLean Golf School
at the Wigwam Resort
Litchfield Park, Ariz.

CHECKPOINT

THE PROBLEM
A lot of golfers can't hit the ball squarely because their hands work against each other, not with each other. This usually comes from experimenting too heavily with extremely strong or weak holds.

THE SOLUTION
To make sure that doesn't happen to you, take the following test:

● Grip any club and have a friend insert two tees in the creases formed between your thumbs and forefingers as shown. If one tee points to the right of your grip and the other points to the left [left photo], you've created opposing forces in your hands and you'll limit their ability to square up your clubface and release the club with authority.

● Your goal is to position your hands on the handle so that the two tees line up [right photo]. In this position your hands can work as a single unit and deliver your clubhead to the ball with zero wasted energy.

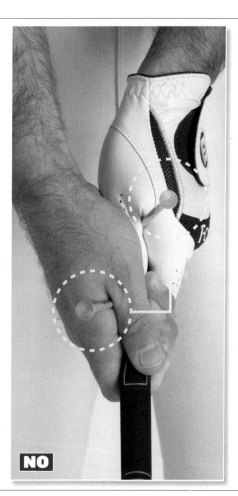

NO

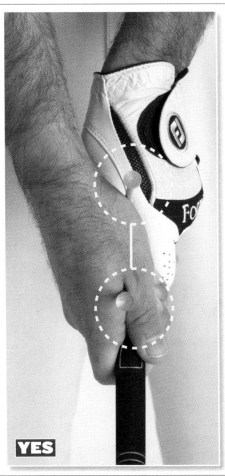

YES

● If you slice, line up the tees over the right side of the grip. This gives you more power to square up the clubface through impact. Line the tees up over the left side of the grip to keep the face from closing too quickly and reel in your hook or hit a purposeful fade.

"Whether you like a strong, weak or neutral hold, make sure your thumb creases line up."

—*Jason Carbone*

TRY THIS!

GRIP YOUR CLUB NATURALLY

Stand up straight with your arms at your sides and notice how your left hand hangs. Some players' hands hang with the left palm facing straight back (like mine, pictured here). Other players' hands hang with the left palm facing the target, with everyone else in between. The point is that everyone's hands hang differently, and the grip that will work best for you is the one that doesn't disturb your natural hand position. Before taking your grip, let your left arm hang and then place your left hand on the handle without changing its position. Now you're set.

—*Top 100 Teacher Dan Pasquariello*

How to Step Into Your Shot

"I miss my targets even when I think I've made a good swing. How can I aim better?"

"Follow this step-by-step guide to take perfect aim every time."

SCOTT MUNROE
Adios Golf Club
Coconut Creek, Fla.

THE PROBLEM
You stand behind the ball on the tee box and pick your target, then take your stance just like you're supposed to. So why does the ball land right of your target, and sometimes miss it by a country mile, whether it's a spot on the green or the middle of an extra-wide fairway?

THE SOLUTION
When you take your stance, you tend to align your body to the target. But since your body sits to the left of your ball-to-target line, aiming your body at the target means you're aiming your clubface to the right. Follow the steps at right to stop wasting strokes due to poor alignment.

1
Stand behind the ball and select a target on the green (where you want the ball to land). Draw a line from your target back through the ball.

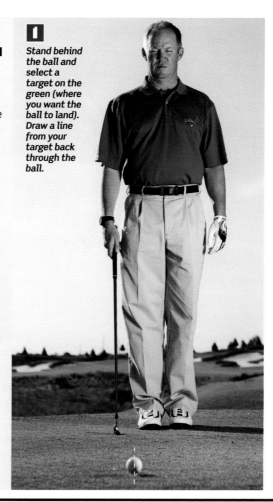

2

Take a sizable— yet easy —sidestep to your left.

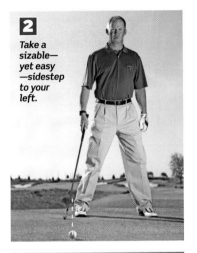

3

Pick a new target, parallel to your original target line, and walk down your new line.

CHECKPOINT

CHECKPOINT

TRY THIS!

STAND THE CORRECT DISTANCE FROM THE BALL

Make a fist. The width of your fist is how much space there should be between your body and the butt end of your 5-iron. The longer the club, the farther you should be from the ball. For a driver, the ideal distance is a fist plus your thumb; for a wedge, about half a fist.
—*Top 100 Teacher Mitchell Spearman*

4

With your eyes on your original target, step forward and place your right foot on your second target line and point the clubface down the first.

5

Now set your left foot—your eyes should still be on the original target. Your body is now aligned parallel to your clubface—you won't miss this shot right.

For a 5-iron, maintain about a fist-width gap from your thighs. For a driver, it's a fist plus your thumb.

"My stance feels okay, but how do I know I'm setting up in the right way?"

"Find a mirror and check your address position for these critical features."

CHECKPOINT

CHECK THIS!

Take your address position in front of a mirror (or solicit the help of a trustworthy friend) and copy the positions you see here. Get these down and your swing will take care of itself.

1. You should see that your right shoulder is lower than your left, your hands are even with the ball, and the Vs of your grip point to the right side of your face.

2. Take a balanced, shoulder-width stance using your heels—not your toes—as a guide

3. With good posture, your knees, hips and shoulders are spaced equally apart, like the rungs on a ladder.

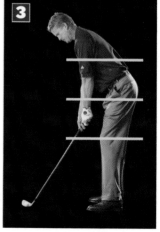

2

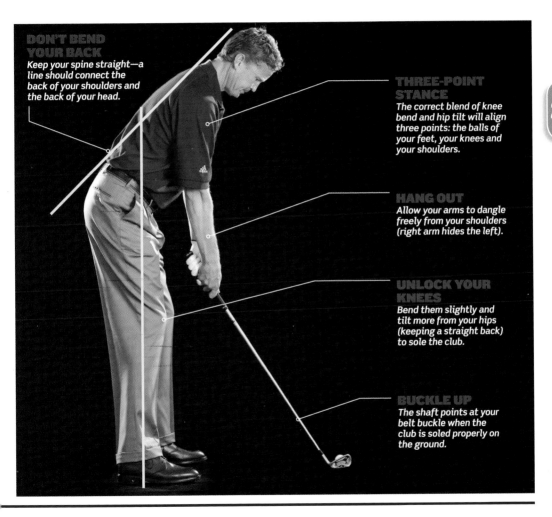

DON'T BEND YOUR BACK
Keep your spine straight—a line should connect the back of your shoulders and the back of your head.

THREE-POINT STANCE
The correct blend of knee bend and hip tilt will align three points: the balls of your feet, your knees and your shoulders.

HANG OUT
Allow your arms to dangle freely from your shoulders (right arm hides the left).

UNLOCK YOUR KNEES
Bend them slightly and tilt more from your hips (keeping a straight back) to sole the club.

BUCKLE UP
The shaft points at your belt buckle when the club is soled properly on the ground.

How to Find Correct Posture

"I don't know what good posture is supposed to look like. Please help."

"Follow these four steps to create perfect setup posture and a consistent swing."

SCOTT SACKETT
McCormick Ranch GC
Scottsdale, Ariz.

DO THIS!

The body angles that you create at address determine what you can and cannot do in your swing. Bad address angles leave you with the type of inconsistent contact that's been ruining your scores.

STEP 1
Step up to the ball with your feet together and your club in the air in front of you. Then, open your feet to shoulder width, making sure that the ball is in the proper position in your stance.

STEP 2
Lock your knees and bend from your hips, keeping your shoulder blades back and your spine straight. You're looking for about 30 degrees of forward bend (about when your chin is even with your toes).

2

When you create good angles at address, however, you're in better position to make a good swing. Follow this four-step checklist to get your address position perfect for solid shots.

ROCK YOUR FEET FOR BALANCE

Balanced swings are good swings, and good balance starts at address. Take your normal setup and rock gently forward on your toes, then back onto your heels and forward again so that your weight is evenly distributed across each foot. This simple drill places you in perfect balance and in position to make a solid swing.
—*Top 100 Teacher David Glenz*

STEP 3
Without moving anything else, drop your arms and set your club on the ground. If your clubhead doesn't hit the ground behind the ball, move your whole stance—don't just reach out or pull in.

STEP 4
Unlock your knees and bend them slightly. Don't relax too much—keep your leg muscles engaged. Lastly, tilt your upper body to the right so that your head is behind the ball.

"I'm confused about where to position the ball in my stance. Any hints?"

"Every club has a perfect ball position. The trick is to use your nose as your guide."

MICHAEL BREED
Sunningdale Golf Club
Scarsdale, N.Y.

DO THIS!
Each club in your bag features a unique length and lie angle (the angle the shaft creates when the clubhead is soled on the ground). Because of this, you must vary where you play the ball in your stance to accommodate the dimensions of the club in your hands. As a general rule, the longer the club the more forward you should position the ball in your stance, but the ball should never be left of your left shoulder or right of your nose, regardless of which club you're using for full swings. These photos show an easy way to remember exactly where to position the ball for every shot.

"You stand taller with a 3-iron than with a 7-iron, so it will bottom out later in your swing— that's why you play the ball forward in your stance with longer clubs."

—Michael Breed

DRIVER
Position the ball even with the outside of your left shoulder.

HYBRID/WOODS
Position the ball even with the center of your left armpit

3- THROUGH 6-IRON
Position the ball even with your left ear for long and mid-irons.

SHORT IRONS
Play the ball off your left cheek for short irons and wedges.

How to Set Your Weight

"I know I'm supposed to shift weight when I swing, but what happens at address?"

"Pre-setting your weight is critical. Take off one shoe to feel the difference."

DR. JIM SUTTIE
TwinEagles GGC
Naples, Fla.
2000 Teacher of the Year

CHECKPOINT

THE PROBLEM
You just finished a tough round, where you had trouble off the tee with slices and weak hits and never made good contact with your irons.

THE SOLUTION
The solution to both problems is at hand— or, rather, on your feet. Just take off one shoe to get the feel for wood and iron swings. Here's how:

DRIVER FIX
TAKE OFF YOUR
RIGHT SHOE
If you strand weight on your left leg during your backswing, you'll come in too steep, leading to either a slice or a pull. Take off your right shoe, settle into your address, and feel how your weight automatically moves to your right foot. Keep it there in your backswing, and you'll learn how to make a shallower, inside-out swing—the secret to straighter drives.

IRON FIX
TAKE OFF YOUR
LEFT SHOE

The most common mistake people make with their irons is to come down too shallow and release the club early. The result: weak shots that end up short of the green. If you take off your left shoe, you'll stay more centered over the ball and come down steeper and on top of the ball. The missing shoe helps gets your weight to your left side for ball-first-then-turf contact.

Whichever shoe you remove, your weight will settle over that foot—great practice for both irons and woods.

TRY THIS!

TIE ON A TIE TO LEARN HOW TO GET BEHIND THE BALL

Put on a shirt and tie, or at least imagine that you have. Now bend forward into your golf stance and bump your hips to the left so that your belt buckle moves to the left of the tie. The idea is to move the bottom of your spine, not the top.

Swing to the top and check that the tie hangs farther away from the target than your belt buckle (if the tie is inside your belt buckle you've made a reverse pivot). Try to keep this arrangement as you swing back down to the ball.

—Top 100 Teacher Martin Hall

"**I sometimes freeze at address. Is there a good, reliable trigger to start my swing?**"

"Yes—relax and simply try to keep your hands 'in the box' as you start the club back."

MICHAEL HEBRON
Smithtown Landing GC
Smithtown, N.Y.
1991 Teacher of the Year

TECHNIQUE

CHECK THIS!
At address, notice how your hands fit nicely into a small rectangle [right]. This is your "hands box," and you'll know it's in the right place if you take your stance by bending from your hips so that the shaft is perpendicular to your spine. Make sure that your hands don't leave the box during your takeaway. If they move to the right of the box, you took your club back too far to the inside [below].

WRONG!

ADDRESS

Your hands start in a box...

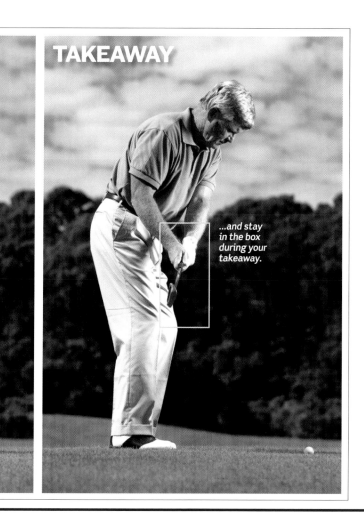

TAKEAWAY

...and stay in the box during your takeaway.

TRY THIS!

TURN—DON'T SWAY—AT THE START

A lot of players think that starting the club back is an arms-dominated event. You'll do much better if you think more about turning your upper body then swinging your arms. Take away the club with your right shoulder while keeping your chin and knees still. This will get your body properly behind the ball and eliminate swaying."
—*Top 100 Teacher Carl Rabito*

Keep your chin and knees quiet.

How to Coil For Power

"When I try to turn my shoulders I shift weight to my front foot. What's the right way?"

"Guarantee a proper, power-rich backswing turn by getting your nose over your left foot."

JOHN DAHL
Oxbow Country Club
Oxbow, N.D.

THE CONVENTIONAL WISDOM

To develop a solid swing that you can repeat, you need to keep your head still during your backswing.

WHY IT'S WRONG

The most natural thing your head can do is float with your body as you coil behind the ball. If you try to keep your head still you'll leave your weight over your left leg. This leads to a reverse pivot, the most common and most damaging power leak.

WHAT YOU SHOULD DO INSTEAD

Here's a good swing thought for your backswing: Your head should move enough so that your nose points at your right foot at the top. If you're in this position, then you'll know that you've transferred your weight to your right side and are in the correct spot to deliver a powerful blow to the ball.

A rigid head leads to a reverse shift.

NO

Allow your head to move far enough in your backswing so that your nose points toward your right foot.

YES

TRY THIS!

TILT AS WELL AS TURN

The secret to a perfect backswing turn is to tilt your shoulders as well as turn them. The right amount of turn and tilt will position your shoulder line on the preferred plane line, helping you apply maximum force and speed to the ball.

Place your driver across the front of your shoulders and turn to the top of your backswing. Check the angle of the shaft after you've fully stretched your upper back muscles against your hips. If you've done it right, the shaft (and your shoulders) will point toward the ground slightly above the ball. Now you're set for power and prepped to deliver all of it to the ball.

—*Top 100 Teacher Jon Tattersall*

WRONG!

If the shaft looks horizontal then your shoulder turn is too flat.

How to Swing the Club Up

"Is it important to get your body behind the ball as you swing the club up?"

"It helps, but it's more important that you brace your right hip to make a stable turn."

MICHAEL HEBRON
Smithtown Landing GC
Smithtown, N.Y.
1991 Teacher of the Year

TECHNIQUE

CHECK THIS!
As you move from your takeaway into your backswing, your main priority is to stay balanced. This means turning *[far right]* instead of swaying, indicated by the fact your head hasn't moved much from address. Also, monitor your right hip position—keep it in place and braced to accept your weight as it moves from left to right. Think of it as the hub around which your body turns. Don't lock your right knee—it'll cause you to weakly lift the club up with your arms.

WRONG!

TAKEAWAY

Keep your head steady...

BACKSWING

...and brace your right hip to accept weight.

TRY THIS!

SYNC UP YOUR ARM SWING AND BODY TURN

As you swing to the top feel like your left arm is connected to your chest. This links your arm swing to your shoulder turn. Take practice swings with a glove tucked under your left armpit. Try to complete your backswing without the glove falling out. It will feel like you're losing power, but limiting the length of your arm swing actually helps you hit the ball better.

—*Top 100 Teacher Donald Crawley*

Keep your left arm connected to your chest for a solid backswing.

"What's wrong with my swing? I never feel solid or coiled at the top of my backswing."

"Too much turn and not enough arm swing, or vice versa. Here's the quick fix."

DR. JIM SUTTIE
TwinEagles GGC
Naples, Fla.
2000 Teacher of the Year

CHECKPOINT

THE PROBLEM

Swing to the top of your backswing and stop. If your **right elbow sits much lower than than your left,** then your club is in a "laid off" position (pointing left of target), and you're set up to come down on a steep, outside path. The result is often a pull or even a shank. (Equally as damaging is the case when your right elbow is much higher than your left, and the club is pointing to the right. This position is called "across the line," and it tends to cause a push or extreme hook.)

THE SOLUTION

In the photo at far right you can see that my **elbows are level and the club is parallel to the target line.** This position promotes a proper swingpath that comes just slightly from in the inside, which is the most direct and consistent path to the ball. The simple fact is if you don't have balanced elbows you're going to have to make compensations. Make level elbows your goal at the top.

Laid off.

Across the line.

Balanced elbows are the key to consistency.

How to Set The Clubface Square

"I spray most of my shots. How can I know my clubface is square?"

"Dial in the correct face angle by bowing or flexing your left wrist. It's important to get this right at the top of your swing."

TIM MAHONEY
Talking Stick GC
Scottsdale, Ariz.

DO THIS!
Slices, hooks and everything bad in between result from your clubface not squaring up to the ball at impact. This happens because you're not square at the top of your backswing, either. Good ball strikers know that if you're square to your path at the top (same clubface and shoulder angles), chances are you'll be square at the bottom.

To check if you're doing it right, swing to the top and hold. If you're a slicer, the clubface is probably pointing at the target. Try varying amounts of left and right wrist bend to match the face angle to your swing path. Ultimately strive for a flat left wrist at the top of your swing. This will take care of what's happening at impact.

OPEN
Adding left wrist cup opens the face and requires perfect timing to get square at impact.

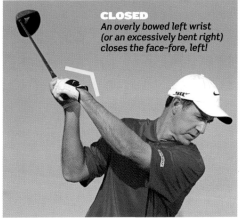

CLOSED
An overly bowed left wrist (or an excessively bent right) closes the face—fore, left!

SQUARE
With very few exceptions, solid ball strikers have a flat left wrist position at the top.

TRY THIS!

DON'T COLLAPSE AT THE TOP

Swinging your club past parallel doesn't mean extra power—it just means you're overswinging, usually because you collapse your wrists and left elbow at the top. To fix this, firm up your grip and try to keep your left arm straight. This doesn't shorten your swing—it strengthens it for real swing power.
—*Top 100 Teacher Mike Davis*

Folding your left elbow is a no-no.

Q

"I can't seem to find the 'slot' on my downswing. My swing is always outside-in. Any help?"

A

"Make the 'Magic Move' by dropping your right shoulder down."

MICHAEL HEBRON
Smithtown Landing GC
Smithtown, N.Y.
1991 Teacher of the Year

TECHNIQUE

CHECK THIS!
If you're solid at the top, most of your work is done. But you can lose it all in an instant if you make the wrong first move down. Check what's happening with your right shoulder. Does it drop down at the start of your downswing? If it does, you're in a great position to deliver the club on plane [yellow box]. If your right shoulder stays at the same height [below], your downswing will be above plane and your chances of a pull or slice will skyrocket.

WRONG!

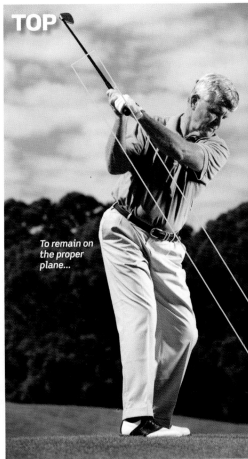

TOP

To remain on the proper plane...

DOWNSWING

...your right shoulder must drop down.

TRY THIS!

PAUSE AT THE TOP FOR A SMOOTHER DOWNSWING

At address, imagine that your shaft is half-filled with water. Before you begin your swing, all of the water is in the bottom half of the shaft, but as you swing to the top gravity pulls the water toward the grip. Instead of racing back down to the ball, allow the liquid to completely fill up the grip end before you start back down. Just that little pause will keep you from lunging or lurching at the ball and make for an overall

smoother motion. It will also stop your hands from starting your downsiwng, allowing your body to correctly lead.

—*Top 100 Teacher Steve Bosdosh*

Q

"I hit the ball straight, but I don't really compress the it. How do I get that impact power?"

A

"The secret is in your wrists, and how you time their hinging and unhinging."

DAVE PHILLIPS
Titleist Performance Institute
Oceanside, Calif.

THE PROBLEM

You tend to pick the ball off the grass, which allows you to hit decent shots,but you never get the feeling of true compression and the ball often falls short of your target.

THE SOLUTION

The only way to generate powerful iron shots is to hit down on the back of the ball and then drive your clubhead through the dirt. While many moves are required to do this on a consistent basis, you can take a giant step forward by focusing on the action of your right wrist. Follow the steps at right.

Hinge here.

STEP 1 HINGE & SUPPORT

As you swing the club to the top, hinge your wrists so that you create a noticeable angle between your right forearm and your right wrist. If you do it correctly, the back of your left wrist will be flat and you'll feel like your right hand is under the club, supporting it rather than directing it. This right-wrist hinge is an important power lever in your swing—without it, your swing can't move at the fastest possible speed.

Hold here.

STEP 2 RETAIN & RELEASE

On your downswing, try to keep the angle in your right wrist intact. The easiest way to do this is to simply leave it alone. Even when your hands swing below your belt, you should still have your right-wrist hinge. If you do it correctly, it will feel like your clubface and your right palm are pointing toward the ball as you enter the impact zone. This is where you'll get max compression.

TRY THIS!

DROP THE CLUBHEAD

Since the handle of the club leads the way to impact, the clubhead should be descending on a slight arc when it contacts the ball. To get a feel for that sensation, try this drill.

1. Push a row of three tees into the ground two clubhead widths behind the ball as shown.

2. Address the ball with a 6-iron and swing. You want to nip the tees on the backswing and then miss them on the downswing.

3. Swing all the way through to the finish. If you miss the tees coming down, the clubhead correctly lagged behind the handle, and you should be admiring a high, straight shot.
—*Top 100 Teacher John Elliott, Jr.*

"I know you're supposed to swing from inside-out, but what exactly does that mean?"

"Picture a clock—your swing moves from 7 o'clock to 1 o'clock."

MICHAEL BREED
Sunningdale GC
Scarsdale, N.Y.

TECHNIQUE

DO THIS!
If swinging correctly from inside-out is difficult for you, or if you can't break your habit of swinging outside-in with your clubface cutting across the ball through impact (see slice, pull, pull-slice), try thinking about your swing path as it relates to a clock. At address, imagine your feet rest at the 9 o'clock position on a clock face. As you swing down from the top, try to sweep your clubhead on a path the crosses 7 o'clock on its approach to the ball, and crosses 1 o'clock after impact. If you slice, you're likely swinging from 5 o'clock to 11 o'clock.

Swing to the one o'clock position on a clock face to groove the right path.

DRILL

BUILD UP "LAG POWER"

Here's how to retain your right-hand angle so you don't release the cub too early and rob your swing of precious potential energy.

Swing.

Stop.

Swing!

STEP 1
Swing any club up to the top and stop. Check that your left shoulder has turned behind the ball with your weight over your right foot. Also, make sure that your left arm is firm and that your right arm is bent 90 degrees.

STEP 2
Swing the club down until your left arm is parallel to the ground and stop. Make sure your right arm is still bent 90 degrees. Don't simply "pull the handle." This important first move down must come with a forward bump of weight.

STEP 3
Straighten your right arm and fire your club through impact. Feel how the piston move puts outward pressure on the handle and keeps your wrists from losing their hinge. The only time both arms are straight is after impact.
—*Top 100 Teacher*
Kevin Walker

"What moves first in my downswing— my lower body or my upper body?"

"Think of it as a sequence, one that involves storing energy and then releasing it."

ANNE CAIN
Anne Cain Golf Academy
Amelia Island, Fla.

TECHNIQUE

THE PROBLEM

You're struggling with accuracy because you're getting lost on your downswing. It's important to think of your downswing as a sequencing of events. The first third of the downswing is all about storing energy and moving the club to the proper plane. The second third of the downswing should be delivering the energy through a strong, late, heavy twist. The last third involves rotating your body and hitting the ball with a square clubface. You're probably executing this sequence in reverse.

THE SOLUTION

Break your downswing into 3 parts, and practice them slowly as shown here.

STEP 1

Go to the top of your swing and stop. Your first move is to drop the club behind your back without moving your hips, shoulders or wrists.

STEP 2

Drop your arms. You did it correctly if your right elbow points inside your right hip. This it's what allows you to set the club and maintain lag.

STEP 3

Now you're ready to hit with max power on the right path. Twist your body to pull the club through. Your hips should be open at impact.

DRILL

TRY THIS!

SHIFT, DON'T SLIDE

Many players try to create power by sliding their hips toward the target. Instead of sliding, make a slight shift and then rotate. To feel the right move, swing a 6-iron with your left arm only. As you start down, shift and rotate your hips and legs forward. You'll feel your left arm fall down your chest. That's the drop you need.

—*Top 100 Teacher Don Hurter*

Feel your left arm fall down in front of your chest.

"Sometimes I strike it well, other times my impact feels mushy. How can I make a more consistent compression?"

"That's easy— move forward so that your swing bottoms out in the right spot."

MICHAEL HEBRON
Smithtown Landing GC
Smithtown, N.Y.
1991 Teacher of the Year

TECHNIQUE

DO THIS!
If you often hit fat or thin shots, pay attention to how far your lower body moves toward the target on your downswing. This forward motion allows your hands to get to the ball before your clubhead, and moves the bottom of your swing arc toward the target so you contact the ball before the ground. If you hang on your right side *[below]*, you'll make contact behind the ball (fat) or after your swing has already bottomed out (thin).

WRONG!

DOWNSWING

Shift your weight forward during your downswing...

2

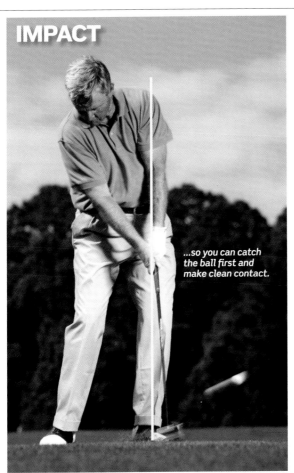

IMPACT

...so you can catch the ball first and make clean contact.

TRY THIS!

STACK UP FOR IMPACT

Set up to the ball with a 7-iron, then pull your left foot back 18 inches and rest it on your toe. Make half-speed swings and note how the awkward stance forces your upper body to remain on top of your lower body (otherwise you'll fall off-balance). That's the sensation you're looking for at impact.

—*Top 100 Teacher Brady Riggs*

Stack your upper body over your lower.

Q

"I don't have a lot of time to hit practice balls. Can I practice impact without going to the range?"

A

"Absolutely. You can do my impact drill at home or in the office to instantly improve your strikes."

ED IBARGUEN
Duke University GC
Durham, N.C.

DRILL

DO THIS!
This simple drill makes it easy to improve your ball striking, and you don't even have to hit a ball.

STEP 1
Take your normal address position and extend your left arm straight away from your shoulder. Keep your wrist flat and make a hook with your index finger.

STEP 2
Slide your right arm underneath your left arm so that the backs of your wrists are touching. Now hook your two first fingers together (inset photo, above), matching up the first joint of each finger.

STEP 3

Make your usual backswing. You'll notice that the end position of your backswing will be a lot shorter than normal. This is because your left arm can only swing back so far before it begins to bend or you begin to stand up out of your original address posture.

This simple drill stops your backswing in the right spot and sets your hands in the ideal impact position.

STEP 4

Swing your arms down to your pre-impact position (photo, left). Notice how all of your moving parts are together and coordinated. Pause for a moment when your hands are over the imaginary golf ball. This correct hand position means that the shaft will be leaning forward when the clubhead is still 18 to 24 inches from the impact. Here your right wrist remains bent backward, your left wrist is still flat and in line with your left arm. Do that in your real swing and you'll catch every shot crisp and with very little chance of slicing.

"If I hit one more weak slice I'm going to quit. How can I drive the ball hard and straight?"

"Here's a swing thought to improve your ball striking: make your left leg a fence post."

PETER KRAUSE
Hank Haney International
Junior Golf Academy
Hilton Head, S.C.

FAULT FIX

THE PROBLEM
You often hit short and right of your targets.

WHY IT'S HAPPENING
If you're inconsistent with your irons like this, you're probably hanging too far back and pivoting around your right leg through impact (instead of your left). This causes you to release the club early and swing with a lifting or scooping motion. The result: High and weak shots.

THE SOLUTION
Start your downswing with your left knee and hip "posting up" on top of your left foot first. This allows your hands and arms to drop down without releasing the club before impact. As your left hip begins to clear out of the way, your right knee and hip move up into the ball, allowing you to deliver the club into the ball with power and accuracy. Once you ingrain this move, you'll start to hit your irons the proper distance and trajectory.

Think of your left leg as a post that your right side can move toward through impact. This gives you the best chance to strike your irons with power and accuracy.

Pivoting around your right leg on your downswing is the fast track to high, weak shots.

DRILL

TRY THIS!

USE YOUR LEFT HAND TO STOP YOUR CHICKEN WING

You chicken-wing. You can't really see yourself doing it because it's happening at the fastest part of your swing—impact—but that bent left elbow in your follow-through is easily diagnosed by the never-ending series of slices and thins you hit with every club in your bag. When most golfers attempt to fix their chicken wing, they go

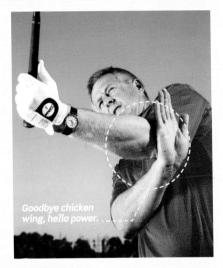

Goodbye chicken wing, hello power.

right to the source: their left elbow. Yes, that's part of the problem, but the main culprit is your body turn, or lack thereof. When your trunk stops rotating at the bottom of your downswing, the clubhead passes your hands and causes your elbow to bend.

To fix the problem, grab your driver with your left hand only and set the back of your right hand behind your left elbow. Make an easy swing with your left arm back and through, applying pressure to your left elbow the whole way. **You should feel a strange sensation as you swing through impact: your left elbow turning down—not folding up—and pulling your upper body into the shot**, which forces you to turn all the way through. Goodbye, chicken wing, hello power. Swing back and through a few times with your right hand behind your left elbow to help groove the feel, then take it to the course. You can even use it as part of your practice swings.
—*Top 100 Teacher Martin Hall*

26 | How to Swing Into a Solid Finish

"Does what happens after impact matter much to my swing?"

"Definitely—If you're not solid in the forward-part of your swing, then what came before was likely off as well. Keeping your posture will help."

MICHAEL HEBRON
Smithtown Landing GC
Smithtown, N.Y.
1991 Teacher of the Year

TECHNIQUE

DO THIS!
Very few golfers consider what happens after impact very important. But the plane on which your club exits the hitting area says a lot about the path you took on your backswing and downswing. If it's to the left [below], you swung outside-in and hit a slice or pull. Try to re-trace your backswing on your through-swing. You'll have to maintain your forward bend until the force of your swing causes you to straighten up in your finish.

WRONG!

IMPACT

Your club enters impact on one plane...

FOLLOW-THROUGH

...and remains on that plane into your follow-through

TRY THIS!

SHAKE HANDS WITH THE TARGET

From some angles it looks like your forearms cross shortly after impact—but that's an illusion. In a proper release, your right hand remains to the side of the shaft. Halfway into the follow-through, it should look like you're shaking hands with someone to your immediate left.
—*Top 100 Teacher Fred Griffin*

Shake hands with the target.

"How much effort should I make in releasing the club after impact—a little or a lot?"

"It depends on your swing. The best advice is to do whatever you have to do to get your left knuckles pointing down."

ROBERT BAKER
Logical Golf
Miami, Fla.

DO THIS!
Make your everyday swing then stop just after impact or when your hands reach hip height. Look at your left hand and see in which direction your knuckles point. If they're pointing to the sky, then you failed to make a proper release.

For maximum speed and distance, gradually rotate your forearms (right over left) and turn your wrists through the hitting zone so that your **left-hand knuckles and left elbow point toward the ground in your release**.

Through the hitting zone, sling the club smoothly past your left thigh by trying to "flick" an imaginary object off your left thumb. Or, think of how you'd turn your left hand out to hitch a ride.

When you need full power and speed, point your left-hand knuckles at the ground.

TECHNIQUE

TRY THIS!

POINT YOUR LEFT KNUCKLES UP FOR OTHER SHOTS

The left-knuckles-down theory is good for all full-swing shots. But some shots, like greenside bunker shots, chips and pitches, knock-downs, bump-and-runs and punch shots, require a knuckles-up approach. That's because they require control over raw distance, with your hands ahead of the clubhead at impact and the back of your left hand pointed up in your follow-through. **For these shots you want to hold off your release,** which is the fastest part of your swing. Through impact, cup your left wrist slightly and lift the back of your left hand toward the sky. This usually produces a scoopy impact, but if you set up with your hands ahead of the ball, your contact will be crisp.
—*Top 100 Teacher Robert Baker*

Hit ultra-accurate short-game shots by pointing your left-hand knuckles toward the sky.

"I think I'm shifting my weight correctly, but how do I know for sure?"

"You've done it right and kept bad shots like slices at bay if you can hide your left knee with your right."

MARTIN HALL
Ibis Golf & Country Club
West Palm Beach, FL.
2008 Teacher of the Year

THE PROBLEM
A big part of the slicing problem is weight shift—the more your weight hangs back on your right side, the more the ball will slice.

THE SOLUTION
You need to get your right side all the way though the ball. As you swing through impact and into your follow-through, try to hide your left knee behind your right knee—a person watching you from across your target line shouldn't see your left knee and upper left leg when you reach your finish. To do this, turn your hips, don't slide them. Another good feeling is to get your right shoulder closer to the target than your left after impact. Weight shift is a full-body event—hiding your left knee helps you correctly transfer all of your weight to your left side during your downswing.

Hiding your left knee with your right guarantees an anti-slice weight shift.

Weight back = slice.

DRILL

HOW TO PRACTICE THE END OF YOUR SWING

If you can groove a solid finishing position first, it'll be easier to make the swing moves necessary to finish in balance and eliminate poor ball flight. Put on a baseball cap and take your normal address position with an iron, then follow these steps:

STEP 1
Take your stance then, without moving your feet, stand straight up and bring your club straight up over the top of your head.

STEP 2
Make a quarter turn to the left with your face, chest and hips pointing at the target and the butt end of the club pointing to your left.

STEP 3
You'll know you're in the ideal finishing position when you feel the shaft lay across the hair on the back of your head where it pokes out from the cap.
—*Top 100 Teacher John Elliott, Jr.*

Q

"I don't feel like I have very good rhythm and tempo, and it's affecting my swing. Any advice?"

A

"Time your wrist cock with your body pivot in your backswing to get smooth from start to finish."

DOM DIJULIA
Jericho National GC
New Hope, Pa.

CHECKPOINT

THE PROBLEM
You often lose the timing of your swing because you either delay or quicken your wrist hinge in your takeaway. These errors destroy the natural momentum of your club going back, and can do the same on the way back down via a late release or one that occurs far too early in the downswing.

THE SOLUTION
Hinge your wrists at the correct time, which varies depending on the iron you have in your hands and the shot you need to play. Adjust the timing of your hinge to create perfect rhythm and tempo.

For more distance with better tempo, time your hinge so that the club is parallel to the ground when your hands reach waist height.

FOR FULL SWINGS WITH YOUR MID-AND LONG IRONS...
Simply maintain the hinge that you established at address during your takeaway. Full swings require a longer body pivot, so hinge less and turn more as you bring your hands to waist height. You know you've done it right if your chest points away from the target and the butt of the club is outside your right leg when the shaft is parallel to the ground.

For half-swing shots inside 50 yards, your right wrist should hinge before your hands pass your right knee.

ERROR ON THE QUICK SIDE

You've been told to keep the clubhead low in your takeaway, which is good advice unless you over do it [below]. Now you're late on your hinge going back, which means you'll be early on your hinge going forward, and you'll hit the shot fat. As a general rule, hinge your wrists sooner and you'll hear the sweet sound of crisp contact more frequently.

FOR HALF-SWING SHOTS...

Make a full hinge before your hands pass your right knee. Short swings from 30-60 yards require much less body pivot, which means your wrists must hinge sooner in your backswing. You've done it right if your chest points at your right foot and the butt of the club is on top of your right leg when the shaft is parallel to the ground.

A late hinge creates a late release.

TRY THIS!

USE "DOWNTIME" ON THE COURSE TO YOUR TEMPO'S ADVANTAGE

If you're like most golfers you make casual, right hand-only swings while waiting on the tee box or in the fairway for the group ahead to clear away. While most of these mini-swings are made with the sole purpose of passing time, they'll ingrain bad habits since you're likely just flipping your club back and through—a big no-no.

Instead, continue to make your mini-swings when the course backs up, but do so with a purpose. Repeat a solid back-and-forth motion with an eye toward removing tension in your arms and hands. Take it a step further and make sure you're rotating your right hand as the club sweeps beneath you. Turn into your follow-through with the toe of your club pointing up. When it comes time to play your shot, you'll be loose and ready to deliver a smooth strike.
—*Top 100 Teacher John Elliott, Jr.*

"**My swing feels solid, but I often miss my targets by a good ten yards. What's going on?**"

"Your shots go where your clubface is pointed at impact. Watch your watch to find the fairway or the green."

JOHN DAHL
Oxbow Golf Club
Oxbow, N.D.

LEARN THIS!

In order to control the direction of your shots, you must control the position of the clubface at impact. Unfortunately, knowing exactly where the clubface is pointing throughout your swing is difficult, but you can do it if you focus on something you can see, such as your wristwatch.

DO THIS!

Unless your grip is way too strong or very weak, the face of your watch points in the same direction as the clubface. So your goal is to get into the habit of pointing your watch at the target at impact. The position of your watch at impact also can help you discover errors in your swing and clubface position. During your next practice session, watch your watch and you'll find out how to hit straighter shots.

Where your watch points, the ball will follow.

SOLID

Straight shots result from squared impact, evidenced by your hands leading the clubface into impact and your watch facing the target.

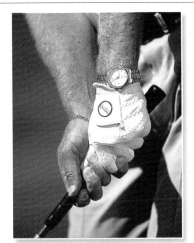

SLICE

If your watch points to the right of the target (or even remotely skyward), the clubface is open, and you're looking at a banana ball.

HOOK

If your watch points behind you, your swing is guilty of too much arm and hand rotation. The clubface is closed at impact, and the ball is heading left.

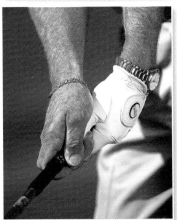

CAST

Great ball strikers have a flat left wrist at impact. If your knuckles get in front of your watch, that's an early release, and you won't know where the ball is going.

"I know what I'm supposed to be doing, but how can I check it other than looking at my ball flight?"

"Use your reflection to see if you're staying on plane throughout your swing."

MIKE LEBAUVE
Westin Kierland
Golf Resort
Scottsdale, Ariz.

YOUR GOAL

To create the perfect swing plane. The perfect plane is described as a circle tilted to match the angle of your clubshaft at address. That's a good visual, but you can't attach a hula-hoop to your 7-iron. All you need to perfect your swing plane is masking tape and a mirror.

HOW TO ACHIEVE IT

Find a full-length mirror and take your address position in front of it. Study your reflection and note the angle of your clubshaft. Place tape on the mirror along this line (we'll call this Line 1), and then another in the opposite direction (Line 2), so that the two lines intersect at 90 degrees. These lines hold the key to grooving an on-plane swing because they help you get your body and club in the correct positions on both the backswing and the follow-through.

Line 1   *Line 2*

1. ADDRESS CHECK

At setup, make sure your shaft mimics Line 1. Your forward bend toward the ball should position your back and head along Line 2. Now you're solid.

2. BACKSWING CHECK

Take your club back to just above waist high and stop. Look at the mirror and make sure your back and head still lie on Line 2 and that your shoulder turn and wrist hinge have placed the clubshaft along Line 1.

If you're not on plane, try turning your left shoulder under your chin and gently cock your wrists a full 90 degrees.

3. FOLLOW-THROUGH CHECK

Swing through impact and stop when your hands reach just above waist height. Study your reflection to make sure that the shaft rests on Line 1, and your head and back haven't strayed from Line 2. The common error here is a clubshaft that lies above Line 1, because most golfers don't swing enough to the left, or if they do they don't execute enough hip turn. You really need both.

Big drives result from widening your swing arc and saving energy for impact. Do both and your swing speed will increase almost automatically.

Technology provides you the tools to knock it out there, but do you know how to use them? Your driver can't swing itself, nor can you simply move your arms or hips faster to create yardage that isn't there. There are hard, fast rules, and since your driver is the longest and potentially most dangerous club in your bag, neglecting them pays off in a triple-whammy of lost yards, balls and strokes.

Once you harness the power of your driver, however, you'll find that playing by the big dog's rules makes the game a whole lot easier. There are three main things you must do to improve your driving distance: increase the width of your swing, sequence your downswing to add club speed, and make contact in the center of the club-face. This section touches on all three, with tips to turn you into a big hitter with accuracy to spare.

3

3

YOU AND YOUR DRIVER

How to turn a love-hate relationship into a
beautiful friendship—and massive yards

Q

"I know that swing power comes from making a big turn, but how do I know if I'm turning correctly?"

A

"You'll know when you're your left shoulder turns into—not under— your chin."

MARTIN HALL
Ibis Golf & Country Club
West Palm Beach, Fla
2008 Teacher of the Year

TECHNIQUE

TRY THIS!
On the practice tee (or while making mock swings in your backyard), place a dollop of shaving cream on the left side of your chin. Make your regular backswing and hold your top position for a count, relax, then check your left shoulder. Is it clean or covered in shaving cream?

WHAT YOU'RE LOOKING AT
The quality of your shoulder turn. If your left shoulder isn't caked with shaving cream, then you rotated your shoulder under your chin (or didn't turn it at all). This kind of shoulder action is devoid of power and results in pop-ups, slices and pulls.

HOW TO ADD YARDS
Try the drill again, and this time make an effort to turn your left shoulder into your chin and transfer the cream on your face to your shoulder. It should feel like you're turning your back to the target and swinging the club back on a slightly flatter plane. These are two important power keys.

Turning under isn't turning for power.

You did it right if you get shaving cream on your shoulder.

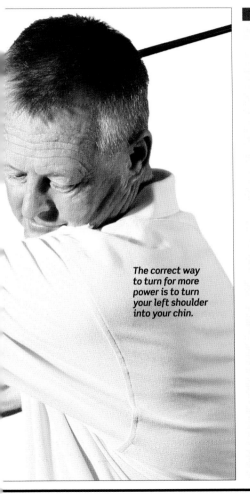

The correct way to turn for more power is to turn your left shoulder into your chin.

TRY THIS!

STRETCH TO 10:30
Move the butt of your club far away from your body

The more distance there is between the butt of your club and the ball when you reach the top, the more room your clubhead has to accelerate on the downswing. When the grip is at 10:30, it's the farthest it should be from the ball. To get it there, swing back while keeping the triangle formed by your shoulders and arms intact. If your grip hits 12:00, your arms probably have folded, collapsing the triangle and reducing your power.

—*Top 100 Teacher Martin Hall*

"The faster I swing, the shorter the ball goes. What gives?"

"Long swings usually mean loose swings, where you lose your swing arc. The secret is to make your arc as wide as it can be."

MIKE MALASKA
Superstition Mountain CC
Superstition Mountain, Ariz.

TECHNIQUE

CHECK THIS!

Look at any great driver of the ball and you'll see that the space between his shoulders is the same at impact as it is at address. You'll never see hunched shoulders or bent arms as the club swings through the hitting zone.

Maintaining the distance between your shoulders creates the necessary room for you to swing through impact and, more importantly, helps you maintain the width of your swing arc for enhanced speed. To establish and better retain width, use the muscles in your back. At address, bring both hands to ear height with your palms facing outward. As you do, sense how the large muscles of your back bring your shoulder blades closer together and pull your shoulders farther apart. Now, bend from your hips into your normal address posture, keeping your back engaged and your blades pinched together. Now you're set for power.

STEP 1
Pinch your shoulder blades together to get wide at address.

STEP 2
Keep your shoulders apart as you settle into your driving stance.

STEP 3
Re-create wide—not shrugged— shoulders at impact.

TRY THIS!

TAKE A HIKE!
Borrow this football move to add even more leverage to your driver swing

Without a club, set your hands like a quarterback ready to receive the snap from center, with the lifeline of your right hand placed firmly on top of your left thumb. That's the pressure you need to maintain the width of your swing (which is determined by the length of your left arm). Make a mock backswing and try to maintain the pressure on your left thumb all the way to the top. You know you've done it right if you feel your right hand push your left arm outward.
—*Top 100 Teacher Tim Mahoney*

Q

"Where's the best place to tee the ball in my stance to make sure I get the most out of my swing?"

A

"Use your left heel as your guide, and the zipper on your pants to get the power tilt you need at address."

ANNE CAIN
Anne Cain Golf Academy
The GC of Amelia Island
Amelia Island, Fla.

TECHNIQUE

THE PROBLEM
Studies show that nine out of 10 players set up on the tee box with the ball too far back in their stance. **If the ball is even one inch too far back in your stance, your drive will fl y 15 to 20 yards right of your target.** This means you need to make power-draining compensations in your swing to hit it straight, including coming "over the top" or "casting" from the top—that is, uncocking your wrists too early—and falling backward in your swing to stay behind the ball. These are serious power drains.

THE SOLUTION
Play the ball off your front heel when hitting driver, with the insides of your feet spread to shoulder width. This positions the ball opposite the tip of your front shoulder, and negates the feeling that you have to swing over the top to make contact. To really make sure you bust it long and straight, **tilt your spine away from the target** so that your left ear lines up with the zipper of your pants. For irons, narrow your back foot a half inch per club. All you change is stance width. Everything else stays the same.

Always position the ball off your front heel with your feet spread so the insteps are under your shoulders. Position it too far back and you'll lose distance and accuracy off the tee.

WRONG!

RIGHT!

CHECKPOINT

TRY THIS!

GRIP WITH YOUR FINGERS FIRST
A palm grip slows you down

Your hands represent one-third of three power sources in your swing (your arms and your pivot are the other two). To unlock their inherent energy, start by gripping the club in your fingers. Think about a major league pitcher: When he wants to bring the heat, he grips the ball in his fingers. When he wants to take something off a pitch, he holds the ball in his palm. When you hold the club in your palms it limits your ability to release the club. A palm grip also creates tension because you have to squeeze tighter to hold the club, and that dramatically decreases clubhead speed. How important is a finger grip? It's the first thing you should consider in the search for more power.

—Top 100 Teacher Sandy LaBauve

WRONG! A palm grip robs you of speed.

RIGHT! A finger grip adds speed.

How to Set Up for Speed

"I can only swing my arms so fast. Is there a way to add speed when you're already moving as fast as you can?"

"The easiest way to add speed is to drop your right foot back at address."

MIKE ADAMS
Hamilton Farms GC
Gladstone, N.J.

TRY THIS!
On the tee of a long par 4 or par 5 that you can reach in two if you really get a hold of one, drop your right foot back (about a full foot's length) at address.

HOW IT GIVES YOU POWER
Dropping your right foot back allows you to make a bigger shoulder turn during your backswing—the secret to adding yards to your drives. Also, with a bigger shoulder turn—what instructors refer to as a "deep" backswing—you'll be less likely to overswing your arms. When you try to create distance by making a big arm swing instead of a big shoulder turn, you actually hit the ball shorter, because a big arm swing tends to disrupt your weight shift and timing. (If you've hit big drives with a big arm swing in the past, then you've just been lucky).

A longer swing might feel more powerful (notice how far across the line I am in the photo above), but it's not. A bigger shoulder turn, on the other hand, produces true coil and energy, and is also more likely to keep your swing on plane. Pull your right foot back at address [photo, left] and let shoulder power propel the ball down the fairway.

TRY THIS!

ADD SOME WAGGLE POWER
Lighten your grip pressure to make a more fluid swing and get effortless power

When you place your hands on the handle, do it with firm grip pressure, especially in your fingers. Make it just tight enough so that you feel you have complete control of the clubhead, yet are able to move your wrists freely. That's the secret to a good grip: firm hands and soft wrists. The best way to make sure that your grip is firm and your wrists are soft is to waggle the club back and forth. You see Tour pros waggle all the time—and there's a method to their madness. Cock your wrists back and forth a few times, set the club behind the ball, and then swing. Your acceleration will skyrocket.—**Top 100 Teacher Martin Hall**

Waggle your driver back and forth a few times at address to loosen up your wrists and firm up your grip.

"I often get lost of my downswing when I swing hard. Any way to combine speed and control?"

"Use the power of the O-Factor—the Tour way to properly turn your hips—and watch the yards pile up."

ROBERT BAKER
Logical Golf
Miami, Fla.

TECHNIQUE

WHAT IS THE O-FACTOR?

The angle of your hips in relation to horizontal.

HOW TO USE IT

Turn your left hip up and to the left of the target immediately at the start of your downswing—and keep turning it!

WHAT IT DOES

The move is so powerful that it literally pulls your shoulders and arms along for the ride. And since your hips move first, everything else must accelerate to catch up at impact. Using your hips like this is what allows you to hammer the ball with your driver without swinging too hard.

ADDRESS
Set your body like an airplane coming in for a landing, with your left shoulder and left hip above their right-side counterparts, and your spine tilted away from the target.

O-POSITIVE
At address, your O-Factor should be slightly positive. As you settle into your stance, bump your left hip up to set your body at the correct angle.

BACKSWING
Turn against the resistance of your right thigh, not your entire lower body, and make sure you rotate your shoulders and your hips. This allows you to create maximum energy.

DOWNSWING
From the top, turn your hips immediately to the left and, as the club approaches impact, pull your left hip up. This creates whip-like speed and helps drop your club onto the correct plane.

O-NEUTRAL
You're balanced and loaded up with power if your hip angle shifts back to zero while your spine remains tilted away from the target.

O-POSITIVE
Kick in your right knee to get your left hip moving up and your right shoulder moving down.

3

"I'm looking for a few extra yards. Any easy adjustments I can make without messing with my technique?"

"Try a narrow stance—it works! Keep your feet at hip width to bust big drives."

MIKE ADAMS
Hamilton Farms GC
Gladstone, N.J.

TECHNIQUE

THE PREVAILING WISDOM

A super-wide stance creates the support you need when you're swinging for the fences.

WHY THE PREVAILING WISDOM IS WRONG

When you take a stance with your feet outside your shoulders, your lower legs angle in from your feet to your knees. This is a power-bracing position, not a power-delivering position.

WHAT TO DO INSTEAD

Place your feet under your hips. This "stacks" the upper part of each leg on top of the lower, allowing you to tap the power of your entire leg.

THE EXTRA BENEFIT

A hip-width stance makes it easier to pivot around each hip. This is a fundamental of any striking motion. If your stance is wider than your hips, you'll need to move laterally to get either hip where you need it, and with all that sliding you're bound to reverse pivot and hit a major-league slice. A hip-width stance negates the need to slide and the likelihood you'll slice.

WRONG!
An extra-wide stance encourages sliding.

RIGHT! A hip-width stance improves your pivot.

TRY THIS!

THROW THE HAMMER DOWN
Picture a nail to drive the ball like a Tour pro

Picture a nail stuck into the back of your ball. As you swing down, try to drive the nail through the core. You'll accelerate through the ball instead of to it, generating extra clubhead speed. Focusing on a small target like the head of a nail can also help you deliver the club's sweet spot to the back of the ball more often.

—*Top 100 Teacher Michael Breed*

Accelerate the club through the ball as if you were driving a nail.

"I'm okay with my yardage, but I'm spraying the ball. What can I do to keep my drives in play?"

"Shorten your finish. This quick tip will help you split the fairway every time."

MARTIN HALL
Ibis Golf & Country Club
West Palm Beach, Fla.
2008 Teacher of the Year

THE PROBLEM
Not only do you spray your drives, but you take the anxiety over your sprayed drives to every tee.

THE SOLUTION
Instead of swinging into your normal full follow-through, finish your drives when the clubhead reaches about waist high after impact. Call this spot "Checkpoint Charlie," and go through the following list when you reach it:

- *The clubshaft and your left arm are more or less still in line*
- *Your right wrist is still bent back slightly*
- *Your right arm is across the middle of your torso*
- *Your chest is facing the target*
- *The toe of the clubhead is pointing up, neither too open nor too closed*

If you work on finishing your driver swings with a short follow-through that satisfies the five conditions above, you may lose a little distance, but you'll also land a lot more shots on the short grass.

DRILL

INCREASE YOUR SMASH FACTORS

These two easy drills to teach you to explode through impact

I. GET FROM "INSIDE" TO "ON FIRE!"

While holding a ball in your right hand, extend your left arm and place your driver's head on the ground as shown at right. Now swing your right hand back to its normal position at the top of your swing. From this point, try to throw the ball through the gate created by your left arm and driver shaft (like you'd skip a rock across a lake). Notice how far from the inside you need to come—and how you must keep your spine angle intact—to get the ball through the gate.

2. GROOVE A BIG-TIME SHOULDER TURN

To feel what a strong shoulder turn feels like, grab a medicine ball. Assume your address position and, with your hands on both sides of the ball, make a backswing. At the top, hold it for a count of one, and then try to toss the ball as far left of your target line as possible. The only way to perform this drill correctly is to aggressively rotate your shoulders and, once again, to hold your spine angle.

—*Top 100 Teacher Tim Mahoney*

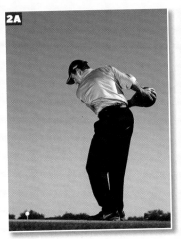

Thanks to technology and our teachers' top tips, you can stretch your scoring zone and get it close with every club in your bag.

Perfect tee shots lead to easy approaches—here's where you can really take your scores low. But sometimes the ball finds a spot that, while smoked off the tee and still on the short stuff, leaves you with an awkward stance, and for most golfers that's a recipe for disaster. Other times your lie is great, but there's an obstacle in your way or the pin is tucked so ridiculously tight that you risk landing in a bunker or water hazard if you go straight at it. The good news is that there's more than one way to get the ball on the green. In fact, there are dozens, and if you acquaint yourself with even a fraction of these options, you'll be prepared for anything the course throws at you. That makes every situation a birdie situation, and separates you from the other golfers just hoping to save par.

4

4

STICK YOUR APPROACH SHOTS

How to get it on and close from every distance and every lie imaginable

"I always come up short when the ball is above my feet. What gives?"

"You won't get as much distance from this lie, so opt for a fairway wood or a hybrid for an easier shot to the green."

ANNE CAIN
Anne Cain Golf Academy
The GC of Amelia Island
Amelia Island, Fla.

TECHNIQUE

THE SITUATION
Your tee shot came to rest on a sloping section of the fairway. When you take your stance the ball is above your feet.

THE PROBLEM
The slope will force your ball to the left. Also, if you make your normal swing, you'll come in too steep and your swing will bottom out before the ball, which causes fat shots, thin shots and all sorts of other bad results.

THE SOLUTION
First, take the right club. For a long approach shot, grab a fairway wood or a hybrid and aim about 10 yards right of your target. If you're playing a short iron, you'll need to aim 15-20 yards right of the target because irons tend to hook far more than fairway woods and hybrids. Make sure to swing more around your body to match the slope of the hill—your normal upright swing will come in too steep.

BATTER UP! When the ball is above your feet, think "baseball swing" instead of "golf swing."

POWER DOWN Go at this one at about 80% speed. If that means using a longer club, then use it.

OFFSET SLOPE Aim 10 yards right of your target to offset how the slope will pull your shot to the left.

HOW TO CRUSH A BALL ABOVE YOUR FEET

DON'T DO THIS!

The secret to executing this shot is to match your swing plane to the slope. The lie angle on a typical fairway wood combines with the slope to produce a much flatter swing plane. Rise above it and you'll have to make too many adjustments on the way down to avoid hitting fat.

The ideal swing plane flattens out on a slope because the hill decreases the effective lie the club.

DO THIS!

Swing your club back on a flatter plane. There's not much to the shot other than making sure you don't come in too steep. Since swing plane is a difficult concept, it's helpful to think about swinging a baseball bat. Feel like you're swinging around yourself. Follow the orange line, not the white one [right].

Stay below your normal swing plane.

"I feel very uncomfortable when the ball is below my feet—I always feel like I'm going to top it. Any advice?"

"Here's a simple tip: Get down, down, down to get this one on."

MIKE LOPUSZYNSKI
David Glenz Golf Academy
at Crystal Springs Resort
Franklin, N.J.

TECHNIQUE

THE SITUATION

You're within easy mid-iron distance to the green, but the ball sits below your feet when you take your stance. Balance is an issue, but the real problem is that the ball is farther away from you than normal.

THE SOLUTION

Lower your body to the ball so you can make solid contact. Also, aim left. The slope will make this ball curve to the right, and the longer club you use, the more right it will bend.

Swing at 70 percent and take one more club than normal. An easier swing will help you maintain your balance. Plus, they don't call it a longer iron for nothing—that extra half-inch between your 6-iron and your 7-iron will help you get down much easier.

You won't keep your posture if you bend only from your waist.

Bend your knees more with your usual forward tilt.

DON'T DO THIS!
Don't just bend from your waist or hips to get down to the ball. The more your upper body bends down toward the ground the more difficult it will be to hold your posture on your downswing. The likely result: You'll raise up and catch the ball extremely thin or send it squirting off to the right.

DO THIS!
At address, take a wider stance than usual and add more knee flex. These simple moves lower your body and bring you closer to the ball.

STAY PUT
When you swing, your main focus should be to maintain the posture you had at address.

Stay in the shot and try to take a little divot. If you straighten up, you have no chance to get back to the ball.

4

ADJUST AIM
Where you aim depends on the club.

For a 4-iron, you probably want to aim 15 yards more left to offset the effect of the slope. For a sand wedge, you only need to aim a couple of yards left.

REVERSE CHOKE
Make sure you're holding the club at the very end of the handle.

You need every inch of your club to get down to the ball.

"How do I get the ball airborne when it's way below my feet. Better yet, how to I avoid topping the ball?"

"Take your swing to the vertical limit. Stay steep and you'll get the job done."

DONALD CRAWLEY
The Boulders Resort
Carefree, Ariz.

TECHNIQUE

THE SITUATION

You're within easy mid-iron distance of the green, but the ball is on a downslope in the right rough. When you go to take your stance, the ball is severely—as in a solid foot—below your feet. You feel like you're going to shank it right from the start.

THE SOLUTION

First, accept the fact that you might not be able to reach the green from this lie—but you can get close. Like all sloping lies, the key to hitting a good shot when the ball is below your feet is to match your swing plane to the shape of the hill.

GET VERTICAL
Notice how much lower my right shoulder is than my left, and how the opposite occurs during your backswing [photo, Step 2].

This "high-low" shoulder relationship is key to producing a very vertical swing (the kind you need to escape this lie).

STAY DOWN
Raise up on this shot and you'll catch the ball very, very thin.

HOW TO NIP IT FROM WAY BELOW YOUR FEET

AIM LEFT
You're going to produce a ton of left-to-right sidespin from this lie. Aim left of the target (10 yards for a mid-iron, 15 yards for a long iron).

STEP 1
Bend from your hips more than normal to get the clubhead behind the ball. It's a good idea to take a longer club than what you need to help you get all the way down. Aim a good 10 yards left of your target—this ball will fade.

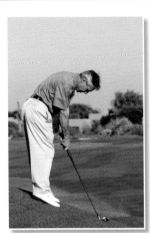

STEP 2
Make as vertical a backswing as possible (it should come easy since you're bent over so much). Feel like your clubhead is riding a Ferris wheel and try to get your hands above your head.

STEP 3
Swing sharply down (as steep as you did on your backswing) and hold your posture—no raising up or dipping down allowed. If you feel the face opening, don't force it closed (you aimed left to compensate for the ensuing fade).

STEP 4
Continue the steep theme in your through-swing, moving the club up sharply after you make contact with the ball. Shift your weight forward from your right-foot toes to the heel on your left foot to maintain your balance.

4

42 | How to Hit a Ball Severely Above Your Feet

"What happens when the ball is almost at knee height? Is there any play here other than a safety punch?"

"Definitely, as long as you make the right mistake. In this case, it's okay to stand up."

BILL FORREST
Troon Country Club
Scottsdale, Ariz.
2006 Teacher of the Year

TECHNIQUE

THE SITUATION
In defiance of gravity, the ball has come to rest on a sideslope. (If the grouds crew mowed more often the ball would have rolled down to a flat lie!) When you take your stance, the ball is higher than your knees.

THE SOLUTION
Many of the keys used to catch the ball when it's just slightly above your feet apply in this situation. Just apply them to an extreme.

This one isn't so tough. Just make sure to plan for the hook ball flight and remain standing tall.

HOW TO BAT IT OFF A HILL

With the ball so far above your feet, your posture will be very tall. (You also may need to choke down on the grip an inch or two.) Check the distance to the green, and take an extra club. The hill will cause your ball to hook, so aim a good 15 yards to the right.

The secret to this lie is to remain standing tall. You can take a full hack if you need to, but the harder you swing, the greater the chances are that you'll lean into the hill to maintain your balance. That's when you catch the ball fat. Try to finish your swing standing as tall as you did at address. To ensure that your swing stays sufficiently flat, think about swinging your right arm across your chest after impact.

WRONG!

Don't use your everyday swing.

RIGHT!

Stay tall and swing your right arm more across your chest.

4

How to Hit the Ball from an Upslope

"It's hard for me to keep my balance on an upslope. What can I do to remain balanced and hit it solid?"

"Relax—this isn't a tough lie. In fact, it's a man-made launching pad!"

STEVE BOSDOSH
The Members Club at Four Streams
Beallsville, Md.

ARM POWER
Gravity won't allow you to move your lower body toward the target like it does on normal lies, so make it an all-arms swing with just a touch of lower-body turn.

BALL IN FRONT
Since the ground is higher on the target-side of your stance, play the ball forward so you won't dig into the hill.

TECHNIQUE

THE SITUATION

Your drive missed the fairway and landed in some light rough. The lie is good, but you're on an upslope. When you take your stance, your left foot is much higher than you're right, and you feel like you're going to tumble down the hill if you make your regular full swing. You don't want to hit a safe pitch back to the fairway because you're just a mid-iron away from the green.

THE SOLUTION

Bag any thoughts of hitting a recovery shot—this isn't a lie that should stop you from getting on in regulation. The adjustments you need to make are easy, including the most important: Hitting two clubs more than the listed distance.

HOW TO SWEEP IT FROM AN UPSLOPE

CLUB DOWN
The hill adds loft. Correctly swinging up the slope does, too, turning your 5-iron, say, into a 7-iron.

Tilt to match the slope.

Stop your hands at shoulder height.

Swing up—not into—the slope.

4

STEP 1
Match the slope
Take a wide stance then shift most of your weight to your right foot. As you do, tilt your body away from the target so that your shoulders, hips and knees match the slope you're standing on.

STEP 2
Short backswing
Make a ¾ backswing keeping your weight on your downhill foot. Any swing longer than this may result in a loss of balance and poor contact.

STEP 3
Follow the slope
Swing down with your arms—you won't be able to shift your weight because gravity is pulling you back down the hill. Swing up the slope and take just a bit of grass—if you take a divot you won't reach the green.

IMPORTANT! Notice how my hips fail to fully open up on this swing. That's gravity holding them back, which is why your arms must do most of the work.

"Downhill plays aren't my strong suit. Is there a move that can help me hit shots from these lies more solid?"

"Try my "down-and-thru" trick. It makes this lie easy and it's good for your regular swing, too."

DONALD CRAWLEY
The Boulders Resort
Carefree, Ariz.

TECHNIQUE

THE SITUATION

You smiled on the tee box when you saw that the hole you're playing ran downhill. The slope added an extra 15 yards on your drive. Standing in the fairway, however, you're not so happy—your lie is tilted just enough toward the target to give you fits. You don't feel very comfortable over the ball when your left foot is lower than your right.

THE SOLUTION

Since the slope you're on isn't too severe, you only need to fine tune your setup and swing. That being said, don't take these alterations casually, otherwise you'll hit a worm-burner that won't get all the way to the green.

TURN & BURN
You need a sharp downswing to get down to the ball from this lie, but don't forget to turn your hips.

LOW BLOW
Since you're swinging down the slope, make a lower follow-through with all of your weight on your left foot.

HOW TO KNOCK IT ON FROM A DOWNSLOPE

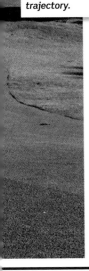

STEP 1

Match your body to the slope. You can do this one of three ways:

CLUB CHOICE
This lie subtracts loft. Swing one club less—it'll give you the same distance but with a softer trajectory.

• Take your address with the ball in the middle of your stance and raise your right foot. Why? To force your upper body to tilt to the left like it should.

• Tip your upper body to the left so that your shoulders match the slope. To check, lay your club across the chest and make sure the shaft tilts with the hill.

• To know for certain that you nailed your posture, line up your club with the buttons on your shirt. If the shaft points at the ball, you're solid.

4

STEP 2

Take the club back along the slope. Since the ground behind the ball is higher than the ground in front of the ball, your backswing will be steeper than what you're used to.

STEP 3

Swing down the slope while turning your hips so that they're open to the target at impact. If you come down steep without pivoting your lower body, you'll jam the club into the ground.

"What do I do when I'm on a really sloping hill? More club? My shots tend to balloon from this lie."

"You need to think 'power' on this one. If you like to hit high draws, this is your lie."

DONALD CRAWLEY
The Boulders Resort
Carefree, Ariz.

TECHNIQUE

THE SITUATION
The ball is sitting up and you have 170 yards to the green. The only problem is that the ball is resting on a severe upslope. When you go to take your stance, your left foot is several inches higher than your right.

THE SOLUTION
First, realize that there are much worse situationsto be in. You're better off being here than facing a severe downslope [pages 108-109]. From this lie, you're allowed to hang back on your right side. Normally, this produces a block. Here, it gives you a nice, soft draw with plenty of punch.

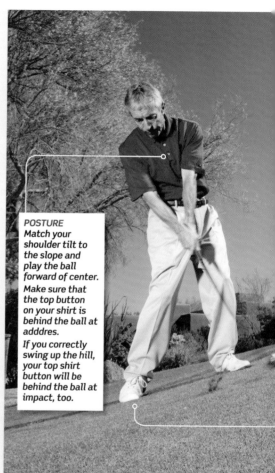

POSTURE
Match your shoulder tilt to the slope and play the ball forward of center.

Make sure that the top button on your shirt is behind the ball at adddres.

If you correctly swing up the hill, your top shirt button will be behind the ball at impact, too.

Make a full shoulder turn going back to encourage a sweeping through-swing that travels up the hill.

HANG & HOLD
Hang back on your right side until the momentum of your swing pulls you into your finish.
Power this swing with mostly your arms, and keep your right shoulder behind the ball at impact.

CHECK YOUR LOFT!

On a flat lie with the club soled evenly on the ground, you're able to strike the ball with the exact amount of loft built into the clubface.

On a severe upslope you can see how loft is added to your clubface. You may need to drop down two clubs to produce the right distance. And since the ball is forward in your stance, there's more time for the face to close. What you end up with is a high draw.

4

"It's hard for me to even take a stance when I'm on a severe downslope. What's the secret?"

"There are actually 5 'secrets' to success from this lie. Nail each one and this shot is a no-brainer."

TED SHEFTIC
Bridges GC
Abbottsville, Pa.

TECHNIQUE

THE SITUATION

The ball has hung up on a steep downslope. When you take your stance, your left foot is *waaay* below your right. Although you have difficulty keeping your balance, you want to play a full shot because you're only a mid-iron away from the green.

THE SOLUTION

Follow the 5 keys here and you'll be in business. Before you swing, however, aim 5 to ten yards to the right (this lie causes the ball to go left) and take at least one extra club (the ball won't go as far since you won't be able to take your full cut).

1. STEADY HEAD
Try to keep your head as steady as possible and stay down on the shot.

3. STAY FLEXED
Keep your right knee flexed. The moment it straightens is the moment you lose all chances of solid contact.

4. SET A BASE
Pull your right foot back 6 inches—it will improve your balance, especially in your follow-through and finish.

TOUGH SHOTS

WHAT TO DO WHEN THE BALL IS BELOW YOUR FEET AND ON A DOWNSLOPE

Use hip power to beat the most difficult uneven lie in the game

Is this lie even legal? Even club selection is a headache. The downslope suggests you use less club because of the de-lofting effect of the hill. Experience, however, tells you that you need more club since the ball usually fades when it sits below your feet. The trick is to determine which factor will have a greater influence on your ballflight. In other words, take an educated guess. The secret to producing crisp contact from this lie—any sidehill lie, really—is to adjust to the slope and lie using your hips, not your shoulders. Copy the setup position here.

• Since the ball is below your feet, thrust your hips back so you can bend over more and get the club all the way down to the ball.

• In addition to pulling your hips back, tilt your right hip up so that your beltline matches the slope.

• Feel how your hips set you up to swing steep and from the inside.

2. MAKE IT STEEP
Swing the club from a very high position in your backswing to a very low position beyond the ball.

5. LEAN FORWARD
Keep the ball in the center, get your knees leaning toward the target and anchor your weight over your downhill foot.

4

"I'm either too long or too short when hitting to a downhill green. How can I hit it the right distance?"

"You've got to know the actual distance of your shot, not just the yardage to the green."

DAVID GLENZ
David Glenz Golf Academy
Crystal Springs Resort
Franklin, N.J.

TECHNIQUE

THE SITUATION

You're in the fairway roughly 140 yards from the pin. Your lie is good. The only trouble is that the green sits below your spot in the fairway. Common sense tells you that you're going to get more out of your 8-iron than its usual 140 yards, but you're not sure exactly how much. You're not even sure if you need to club down.

THE SOLUTION

The best thing you can do in this situation is to follow a well-accepted general rule: Take one club less for each 30-foot drop in elevation. For example, to hit a downhill approach to a green that sits 60 feet below your lie, take two full clubs less. To really nail your club and shot selection, however, follow the three steps at right.

Take one less club for every 30-foot drop in elevation.

1: CHECK THE DROP
Eyeball how far the green sits below you and take one less club for every 30 feet of drop. If you don't know what 30 feet of drop looks like, check the Extra Lesson at far right.

2: CHECK THE PIN
Is it front, middle or back? For a back pin, you'd rather be a little long than short, and vice versa for a front pin. Remember that the ball will be coming in at a steeper angle, meaning it will stop quickly once it hits.

If you're unsure about the club you should use, opt for the longer one and use a 3/4-swing.

3: CHECK YOUR EGO

Before you make a full swing with a shorter club, consider going after the ball with a longer club and a three-quarter backswing. The longer club gives you a greater margin for error in that you don't have to catch the ball perfectly on the sweet spot, whereas with the shorter club you have to absolutely pure it (and how many times do you do that?).

TRY THIS!

HOW TO EYEBALL THE DROP

Stack flagsticks" to get your true yardage

The old rule of "1 less club for every 30 feet of elevation change" holds true, but do you really know what 30 feet of elevation change looks like? Not many do, so forget about elevation drops. What you're really after is the true distance to the flag, and here's how to get it.

Look at the flagstick and calculate how many of them you'd have to stack up on top of each other until the top one was even with your ball (or, if you're below the flag, how many flagsticks would make your ball even with the hole). Take this number and multiply it by eight (roughly the height of a flagstick in feet), and then take that total and divide it by three to give you a number in yards. Subtract that number from the listed yardage to a green that's below you (or add it to the listed yardage to a green that's above you) to discover the true distance. Make your club selection based on that yardage like you would from a level approach.

DO THE MATH!

LISTED YARDAGE: 150 yards
Flags stacked: 3
Drop in feet (3 x 8 feet): 24 feet
Drop in yards (24 / 3): 8 yards
Adjustment: 150 – 8
ACTUAL YARDAGE: 142 YARDS

"It seems like most greens are elevated, which means I'm always coming up short. Any advice?"

"There's more to this shot than simply clubbing down. Here's the pro way to stiff an uphill approach."

DONALD CRAWLEY
The Boulders Resort
Carefree, Ariz.

TECHNIQUE

THE SITUATION
You're at your favorite mid-iron distance and your lie is perfect. Your only concern is that the hole plays uphill. You don't want to come up short because your chipping and pitching so far this round has let you down.

THE SOLUTION
After calculating the true distance to the pin and the correct number of clubs to drop down (see previous page for a foolproof way to get this right), make a smooth, confident swing. There isn't much more to this lie than that, as long as you don't make the typical mistake and under-club yourself.

CHECK THIS!
Look at what the flag is doing. There might be wind above you that you can't detect because you're in a low spot.

DON'T UNDER CLUB
The shortest club you should consider is the one that will get you to the center of the green, even if the pin is up.

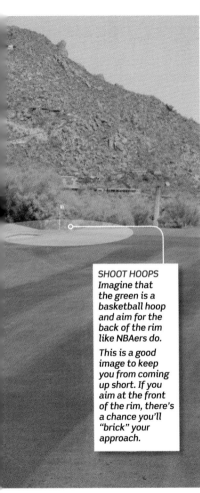

HOW TO HIT AN UPHILL GREEN

If your club selection is correct, a solid swing will get you home. If you need to think about something, focus on making contact with the bottom of the ball. The worst thing you can do here is fall back and scoop the ball into the air. Copy these impact positions:

1 Make contact with the bottom of the ball (that means digging up turf).

2 Load the majority of your weight over your left foot.

3 Head even with the ball.

4 Shaft and left arm form a straight line.

SHOOT HOOPS
Imagine that the green is a basketball hoop and aim for the back of the rim like NBAers do.

This is a good image to keep you from coming up short. If you aim at the front of the rim, there's a chance you'll "brick" your approach.

DON'T DO THIS!
Just because the green is up a hill doesn't mean you need to help the ball into the air. Scoopy impact here means your next shot will be a tough 30-yard pitch.

DO THIS!
Play the ball in the center of your stance and lean the shaft toward the target (set your hands on the inside of your left thigh). Get a sense for what this position feels like and try to re-create it at impact.

"Recently I hit a good drive into a divot. I duffed it and made bogey. What could I have done differently?"

"Beat this bad break with a good setup. Then go find the guy who didn't fill it."

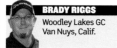
BRADY RIGGS
Woodley Lakes GC
Van Nuys, Calif.

THE SITUATION
Your ball has come to rest in the back of a divot in the fairway, leaving the bottom of the ball below the lead edge of your clubface. Unless you make some adjustments, you'll catch this shot thin.

THE SOLUTION
Take one less club than for a normal lie and follow the steps at right.

LOW RIDER
When the ball is in a divot, its bottom lies below the level of the grass—and the bottom of your clubhead. You'll need a steeper-then-normal downswing to get down to the ball and guard against skulling it.

GET DIRTY
When you're finished with this shot, the back of the divot you were in should be deeper than the front. That means you properly hit down on the ball. Try and create an exposion of dirt.

HOW TO BEAT A BALL IN A DIVOT

STEP 1

Play the ball an inch or two inside your right heel and set your hands even with your zipper. **This leans the shaft toward the target** and de-lofts the clubface (that's why you took one less club—the ball will run when it lands). Place most of your weight over your front leg.

STEP 3

On your downswing, resist the urge to unhinge your wrists and throw the clubhead at the ball. Instead, pull your arms down and let the clubhead lag behind your hands. **Your goal is to collide with the ball rather than pick it clean.** Your follow-through is fairly insignificant. Once you've made contact, forget about your arms and just turn your hips toward the target.

STEP 2

Hinge quickly on your backswing to **set the clubhead higher than your hands,** and keep your weight over your left leg. This creates a steep downswing that will get the clubface to the equator of the ball.

Note how the hands are always ahead of the clubhead.

4

"When I'm between two clubs should I use the smaller club and swing harder, or vice versa?"

"It depends. Here's how to make the right choice and stiff it when you're torn between two of your irons."

STEVE BOSDOSH
The Members Club at
Four Streams
Beallsville, Md.

TECHNIQUE

THE SITUATION
As you step off the yardage to the green you discover that you're 5 yards farther than what you can comfortably hit your 7-iron and 5 yards shorter of what you usually get from a good swing with your 6-iron.

THE SOLUTION
Taking yards off or adding yards to the distance you hit each iron in your bag is an important skill. If you don't have it, then you'll get the ball close to the pin only when it sits at 8 distinct distances (one for each iron you carry), and the chances of that happening aren't very good. Check the clues at right to help you decide between a hard shot with a shorter iron or a soft shot with a longer one, then consult the sequences at far right for how to pull off each one.

Hit the longer club if...
• *The hole plays uphill.*
• *Wind is at your face.*
• *There's trouble short.*

Also, make sure the distance you're sitting at is to the pin, not the center of the green. If you only know the distance to the center, play the longer club if the pin is middle or back.

Hit the shorter club if...
• *The hole plays downhill.*
• *Wind is at your back.*
• *There's trouble long.*

If you only know the distance to the center, play the shorter club if the pin is in the front.

When hitting a longer club, choke up an inch or two on the handle. This shortens the club and makes it easier to control.

HOW TO ADD 5 YARDS TO AN IRON

STEP 1
Play the ball just back of center and lean the shaft forward. This turns your 7-iron, say, into a 6.5-iron.

STEP 2
Make a full backswing. Feel like you're going to pinch the ball between the clubface and the grass, not pick it off the turf.

STEP 3
Accelerate to a full finish, with your body facing the target and your weight over your left foot.

HOW TO SUBTRACT 5 YARDS FROM AN IRON

STEP 1
Play the ball forward, just off your left heel, and set your hands directly above the ball.

STEP 2
Make a ¾-backswing (stop your swing when you feel your hands reach shoulder height).

STEP 3
Without changing speeds, swing to a ¾-finish (make sure you turn fully toward the target).

51 | How to Cheat the Wind

"I fear shots into the wind. The breeze makes me tense. What's the correct way to negate its effects?"

"Hit this low-boring bullet. Even a stiff breeze is no match for it's penetrating ball flight."

TED SHEFTIC
Bridges GC
Abbottsville, Pa.

TECHNIQUE

You might think about making your normal swing with an extra club or two, but the normal loft of even a 5-iron might be too high (the wind will quickly stop any lofted shots in its tracks). Better players play the knockdown shot, a controlled, low-flying half-swing that stays below the wind and travels straight at the target. The knockdown also is a good play any time you need to keep the ball low.

ADDRESS
Play the ball back in your stance—directly off the toes of your right foot.
If your normal grip pressure is a "7" on a 1-to-10 scale, might it a "9" here.

BACKSWING
Make a shorter, more compact backswing (notice how this doesn't mean restricting your shoulder and hip turn).
Feel like your left arm is connected to your chest.

HOW TO KNOCK IT INTO THE WIND

Take two extra clubs (a 6-iron if you're at your 8-iron distance) and follow the steps below. The ball won't spin much, but you can still play the full distance to your target because the wind will stop the ball quickly once it hits on the green. Some players use the knockdown when they're hitting with the wind at their back so the breeze can't carry the shot too far. The most important thing to do in windy conditions is to negate it, and the easiest way to do that is to keep the ball low, whether the wind is coming from behind you or blowing directly into your face.

DOWNSWING
Try to keep your left arm firm. Use your body to move your straight left arm from a horizontal position [photo, left] to a vertical position at impact. Don't go soft on this shot!

4

FINISH
Just like you did with your backswing, abbreviate your finish, but make sure that your head, chest, hips and knees are facing the target. The ball will come out low and hot—it will rise a little but settle quickly once it hits the turf.

"I'm a good wedge player, a decent mid-iron player, but struggle like a novice with the longer clubs. Please help!"

"Try these easy moves to become deadly with your 4-iron on down."

CHUCK WINSTEAD
The University Club
Baton Rouge, La.

THE SITUATION

You're in the fairway but a good distance—at least 180 yards—from the green. A hybrid or fairway wood is too much club. You need a solid 3- or 4-iron into the green and you don't hit these clubs solid very often.

THE SOLUTION

Most golfers struggle to hit crisp long irons because they swing a little too steep and a little to out-to-in. This works well with short irons because they have more upright lie angles. Long irons are built much flatter, so when you swing them steeply you take a lot of turf and make contact out toward the toe. The secret is to shallow out your angle of attack.

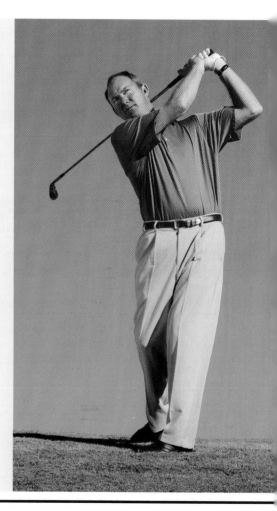

HOW TO SMOKE YOUR 4-IRON

STEP 1

Tilt your upper body to the right at address. Get the buttons on your shirt to the right of your belt buckle.

STEP 2

At the start of your downswing, move your right shoulder toward the ground. Feel like gravity is pulling it straight down. Don't swing your right shoulder out toward the target.

STEP 3

End your swing with a "high finish," with your hands above your head and the clubhead below your hands. If you're high at the finish, it means you were low (shallow) through the hitting area.

Hands higher than clubhead.

Drop your right shoulder down to start your downswing.

4

"I'm okay with flier lies, but struggle when the grass is growing away from the target. Any hints?"

"Getting on gets tough when the grass bends away from the target. You need a steeper swing."

JASON CARBONE
Baltusrol CC
Springfield, N.J.

TECHNIQUE

THE SITUATION

You blocked or pushed your tee shot into the second cut of rough. When you get to the ball you're pleasantly surprised—the lie isn't that bad and you only have 140 yards left to the pin. Forget about playing a wedge back to the fairway—you're getting this baby on!

THE SOLUTION

Step 1 is to check the lie. If the grass is growing away from the target, you have serious issues to consider. Because the direction of the grain is opposite the direction of your swing, the grass is going to slow down your clubhead, grab the hosel and shut the clubface. Sounds tricky, but executing this shot is 90 percent setup.

LIE CHECK
If the grass is growing away from the target, take one more club than the distance and set up to make a sharp up-and-down swing.

STEEP ATTACK
Stand closer to the ball and use extra wrist hinge to produce a steep downswing. The steeper your swing, the less time the grass has to slow down your club and/or close the face.

DON'T BRUSH
The more you think about sweeping or brushing the ball off the rough, the more likely you'll come up short of the green. Save your flat approach for another swing.

HOW TO GET IT SMASH AGAINST THE GRAIN

STEP 1

Stand a little closer to the ball and play it slightly back of its normal position wth the club in your hand. Standing closer will help you swing the club more up-and-down and reduce the time it spends in contact with the grass. Open the clubface a few degrees to offset the shut-down affect of the grass and grip the club tighter than you normally do.

STEP 2

Most golfers try to swing upright by lifting their arms without turning their shoulders. You won't get the ball all the way on with that kind of swing. Just make your regular motion but with extra wrist hinge. Try to point your thumbs at your head as your swing the club to the top [photo, inset]. That will give you the steepness you need to come down sharply on the ball and keep the grass from negating your speed and closing the face.

"I don't have the distance to reach par 5s—and some long par 4s—in two. How do I choose the best lay up?"

"Here's how to play short of the green for birdie, not bogey."

ROGER GUNN
Tierra Rejada GC
Moorpark, Calif.

TECHNIQUE

THE SITUATION
You're playing a long par 5, and while your drive is sitting in the fairway, the green is just too far away to think about going for it in two.

THE SOLUTION
Hit a lay up short of the green. Here you have more options than on any other shot, but if you're like most golfers, you almost always choose the same one: blasting your 3-wood as far as you can. This is the reason you often walk away from a par 5 with a nasty "7" on your scorecard.

HOW TO LAY UP SMART
Before you attempt the longest possible shot (which is the easiest to hit off line, i.e. into the rough or other trouble), consider the 3 questions posed here.

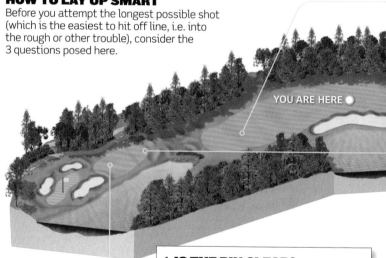

YOU ARE HERE ●

I: IS THE PIN CLEAR?
If the pin is in a favorable center position with no trouble in front, go ahead and blast away with your 3-wood. Pick a precise landing spot and make a smooth, controlled swing—don't try to "kill it." You'll have an unobstructed chip to the hole.

CHECK THIS!

Just because this is a lay-up doesn't mean you can cut corners. Make practice swings and treat it like any other shot.

3: WHAT'S YOUR FAVORITE CLUB?

If your distance control on full-wedge shots is inconsistent, but you always hit your 8-iron 140 yards, then pick a lay-up spot 140 yards from the green. Focus on that landing area as though it were the actual green. Laying up is a numbers game, and you want to hit yours on the money.

2: IS THE PIN PROTECTED?

With the pin behind a bunker on a firm green, being 20 to 30 yards away is not a good spot. You're not far away enough to put enough backspin on the ball to stop it, so even if you pure your second shot with a 3-wood, you're out of position. Select the club that will leave you with a full pitching wedge into the green.

LAY-UP ROUTINE

LAY-UP ROUTINE

Take these steps to avoid that "mind drift" that comes on most lay-up shots:

1 Play to a target, not just a yardage. Visualize a green and flagstick covering your lay-up spot.

2 Go through your pre-shot routine. Start behind the ball, take a practice swing, and treat it like any other shot.

3 Think "lay-up" from the beginning. Do it before you tee off. If you prepare yourself for a lay-up from the start, you won't be disappointed when the time comes to hit one.

Even the best players on Tour miss five to six greens a round. Unlike you, however, they rarely make five or six bogeys. A solid short game turns potential disaster holes into easy pars.

Some days your full-swing shots just can't miss; other times you can't hit greens even from a perfect lie with your favorite club. That's when your short game shows how important it is. Those mild-mannered chips, pitches and lobs make up for poor shots in a hurry, taking you from parts unknown to a comfortable spot next to the pin with swings that rarely go above knee height.

There are thousands of ways to get the ball close from short range, but this section focuses on the simple shots that always get the job done. Mastering these basic short-game plays arms you with enough options to tackle anything the course throws at you. Plus, by the time you have these short shots down pat, you'll understand the adjustments you need to make when facing more difficult situations.

5

5

GETTING UP AND DOWN

Whether it's a precision pitch, a delicate greenside chip or death-defying flop, here's how to get it close.

"I chip well once in a blue moon. What can I do to get more consistent from short range?"

"Borrow from your putting stroke and make chipping simple, clean and easy."

TODD SONES
Impact Golf Schools
White Deer Run GC
Vernon Hills, Ill.

TECHNIQUE

CHECK THIS!

As with most shots, you'll hit better chips if your setup position is correct. The goal of your chipping address is to situate your body, arms, hands and club to create a descending blow without chunking the clubhead into the ground, or striking the ball with the leading edge of the clubface. Your setup and technique are correct if your impact position looks like this:

WRIST FLAT
Your left wrist should be as flat as possible. If you have trouble keeping your left wrist from breaking down, try using your putting grip.

TOE CLOSED
Club turning over on its heel through impact.

WEIGHT FORWARD
Set it there at address and keep it there throughout your stroke. Hanging back leads to thin contact.

SHOULDER DOWN
An easy way to create the desired descending blow is to keep your left shoulder down through impact.

HOW TO SET UP FOR SOLID CHIPS

STEP 1

Aim the clubface at your target, and then raise the club slightly on its toe. This gives you a more upright lie, which makes your chip swing more of a putting stroke. A putting stroke is easier to control because it moves straight back and through. A flatter lie demands you swing the club on an arc.

STEP 2

Move the handle of your club two inches farther toward the target than the front edge of the ball. This de-lofts the clubhead and promotes the downward strike that you're looking for. You can use any wedge with this technique, and even your 8- or 9-iron will work.

STEP 3

The butt of your club should point a couple of inches left of the center of your body. Make sure that your shoulders are square to the target line and your weight is over your left foot, and then play the ball off your right big toe.

STEP 4

Move the club with your arms and shoulders while keeping your hands and wrists quiet and your weight on your left side. As you swing through the hitting zone, you should feel as though you're striking down on the ball while gently closing the clubface.

5

"I often make good chip contact, but my distance control is way off. How can I improve this?"

"Make sure you chip with the handle forward or, put another way, form a 'y'."

STEVE BOSDOSH
The Members Club at
Four Streams
Beallsville, Md.

FUNDAMENTAL

THE PROBLEM
You hit your chips fat so they never get close to the flag, or you blade them over the green.

THE SOLUTION
As you take your address, make sure you set most of your weight over your left foot and move the handle of the club forward. Notice that when you do this your arms and clubshaft form a lower case "y". Establishing this y and keeping it intact during your chipping motion will allow you to come down sharply on the ball and catch it clean before your clubhead makes contact with the turf. Try to "trap" the ball between your clubface and the ground at impact. This will keep your hands forward of the ball and ensure proper contact.

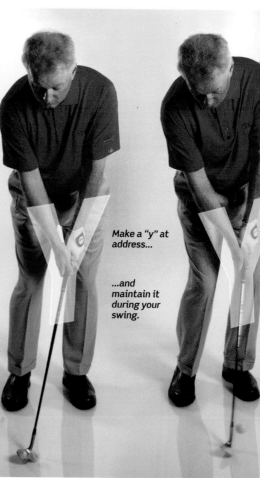

Make a "y" at address...

...and maintain it during your swing.

TRY THIS!

FROM FAIRAWAY OR FROM ROUGH

Change your backswing path to chip it crisp from any lie

Most golfers assume that one swing will get the job done for every chipping situation. In reality, however, you need at least two swings: one for lies in the rough and another for tight lies in the fairway. Here's how to match your ball swing to the situation and leave your chips closer to the hole.

—Top 100 Teacher Brian Mogg

SWING INSIDE FROM A TIGHT LIE

Your goal is to sweep the ball off the turf with a rounded swing. Imagine a shaft stuck in the ground behind your ball and on your target line. Take the clubhead away to the inside of the shaft with very little wrist hinge, as though you were attempting a long putt. Do the same on your forward swing, and then release the clubhead toward the target while keeping your hands at thigh height.

SWING OUTSIDE FROM THE ROUGH

When your ball is sitting down, swing your clubhead outside the shaft on your backswing and hinge your wrists aggressively to get the club up. (Think "low hands, high clubhead.") On your downswing, drop your arms toward the ground and across the ball (left of the target) without releasing your hands. This allows you to dig down deep and pop the ball up without fear of catching it thin.

5

"No matter what I try I can't improve my chipping technique. I'm ready for anything. What can I do?"

"Try using a claw grip. It takes care of many chip-shot errors almost automatically."

KELLIE STENZEL
Atlantic Golf Club
Bridgehampton, N.Y.

FAULT FIX

TRY THIS!

Take your grip in the middle of the handle, but instead of placing your right hand below your left, simply wrap it around your left hand with your right thumb directly over your left thumb. No part of your right hand should touch the grip. Now, make your chipping stroke.

This right-over-left-hand grip removes your right arm from your stroke, making your chip swing a left-arm-dominated motion. This is a good thing, since it's critical that your left arm never stops moving through the shot. If your left arm ever stops moving toward the target on your forward-swing, the clubhead will flip past your hands and you'll catch the shot fat or thin.

The claw grip teaches you proper left-arm action.

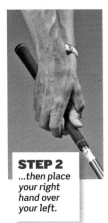

STEP 1
Place your
left hand in
the middle
of the grip...

STEP 2
...then place
your right
hand over
your left.

DRILL

TRY THIS!

ACCELERATE AT IMPACT
Use an old shaft to instantly
improve your chipping contact
and control

Stick a shaft or dowel in the
green at a 45-degree angle a foot
outside your left toe with the grip
pointing away from you *[photo,
below right]*. Set up for a normal
chip then make your best move.
The goal of this drill is to make
clean contact without swinging
past the shaft. You might have
difficulty at first—if you're
like most golfers you tend to
decelerate on the way to the ball,
then speed up after impact once
you feel you haven't given the
shot enough force. (Or you swing
too fast from the get-go and make
too long of a forward swing. In this
case, you're running chips way
past the hole.) Focus
on accelerating to the ball and
giving it a nice pop without
swinging past the shaft. Once
you groove this kind of motion,
you'll find that most of your chips
cover the distance you planned,
and the quality of your contact
will skyrocket.

—*Top 100 Teacher Martin Hall*

POP, THEN STOP
*Accelerating to the
ball then stopping
your swing almost
immediately after
contact teaches you to
get the right distance
out of your chip shots.*

5

"I have a basic chip and a basic pitch. It's not getting the job done. Can you give me some options?"

"Learn two setups and three simple swings to build a Tour-quality short shot arsenal overnight."

BILL FORREST
Troon CC
Scottsdale, Ariz.
2006 Teacher of the Year

CHECK THIS!
Here's an easy-to-remember repertoire of short-game shots would help. All you need to store in your memory bank are two setups and three swings, then pull them up on the course to generate five different trajectories with specific amounts of carry and roll.

SHOT 5
Lofted Pitch
Use it: When you have to carry an obstacle, or when there's little green to work with.

SHOT 1
Low Running Chip
Use it: When you have lots of green to work with, or are playing to an elevated tier.

THE SETUPS

A: CHIP ADDRESS
Play the ball back in your stance and set your hands in front of your zipper. The shaft should lean toward the target. Set approximately 70 percent of your weight on your left foot, and keep it there.

B: PITCH ADDRESS
Play the ball in the middle of your stance. The shaft should sit nearly vertical to the ground. Set approximately 55 percent of your weight on your left foot, and keep it there during your swing.

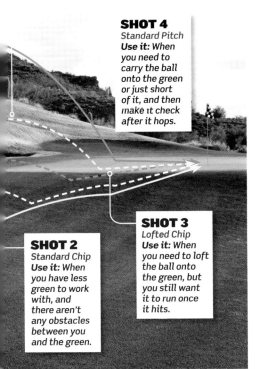

SHOT 4
Standard Pitch
Use it: *When you need to carry the ball onto the green or just short of it, and then make it check after it hops.*

SHOT 3
Lofted Chip
Use it: *When you need to loft the ball onto the green, but you still want it to run once it hits.*

SHOT 2
Standard Chip
Use it: *When you have less green to work with, and there aren't any obstacles between you and the green.*

THE SWINGS

#1: NONE-NONE
(No-hinge backswing, No-hinge through-swing)

Use this for each of the chip shots (Nos. 1, 2, and 3). Make more of a putting stroke than a chip stroke using the same pace both back and through. Hold your wrists firm on both sides of the ball, and keep your hands below your belt line.

#2: SOME-NONE
(Medium-hinge backswing, No-hinge through-swing)

Use this swing for the standard pitch (No. 4). On this swing, hinge your wrists on your backswing, and unhinge them coming back down. This hinging action is what gives your shot height so you can carry the ball farther and control the roll once it lands on the green.

#3: MORE-MORE
(Full-hinge backswing, Full-hinge through-swing)

To generate maximum carry with little roll you need to hinge your wrists on both sides of the ball. This puts maximum loft on the shot, allowing you to carry the ball almost the full distance to the pin. It's the same swing you'd use to hit an explosion shot in a bunker.

HOW TO HIT EACH SHOT

Combine the right club with one of the two setups and one of the three swings to snuggle the ball close.

Swing	1	2	3	4	5
Carry: Roll (%)	25:75	40:60	60:40	75:25	90:10
Club	7-iron	PW	LW	LW	LW
Setup	A	A	B	B	B
Swing	1	1	1	2	3

Q

"I hit a lot of my pitches fat. Other times, I catch the shot thin. How can I improve my contact on short swings?"

A

"It's a lot easier than you think. Try to hit your pitches with your body, not your hands."

ANNE CAIN
Anne Cain Golf Academy
The GC of Amelia Island
Amelia Island, Fla.

DRILL

THE PROBLEM
Most poor pitch shots result from overactive hands and wrists, so keep them calm and instead pitch the ball with your body. Here's a drill that will teach you to rotate your upper and lower body completely through the shot and produce a more consistent launch angle and extra distance.

THE SOLUTION
Place a dowel that's at least 24" (or longer) in the hole on top of your grip and lean the shaft forward at address so the dowel is left of your front hip. Then try to pitch the ball by pulling the club through impact with your body turn, not by flipping your wrists.

NO!
Don't stop turning or get handsy.

YES!
Keep your hands passive—pull them through impact with your body turn.

YOU'RE DOING IT WRONG IF...
The dowel smacks the left side of your torso in your forward-swing.

YOU'RE DOING IT RIGHT IF...
You pitch the ball cleanly and the dowel stays left of your body in your swing.

DRILL

TRY THIS!

A DRILL TO GET EXTRA CRISP

Use this simple drill to play perfect little pitch shots

Most golfers try to lift the ball into the air and end up blading it across the green. Solid short shots are the result of hitting down into the back of the ball, not trying to lift it up. Here's a drill that will produce the kind of pitches you dream about. Balance a club on the top of a water bottle as shown (it's easier than it looks), and place the ball 12 inches behind the middle of the grip. Make your swing without knocking the shaft off the bottle [photo right]. You'll need to descend into the ball and keep your clubhead low to the ground after impact. If you try to scoop the ball or allow the club to pass your hands [photo above], you'll send the club and the bottle flying.

—*Top 100 Teacher Glenn Deck*

Swing down, not up, to avoid a game of pickup sticks.

5

Q

"Sometimes my pitches run out, other times they hit and stop. How can I make them behave like I want them to?"

A

"Consistent pitching comes with consistent contact. Here's how to eliminate the variables."

JOHN ELLIOTT, JR.
Golden Ocala Golf &
Equestrian Club
Ocala, Fla.

SWING THOUGHT

CHECK THIS!

One way to think of your pitch swing is that it's a slightly bigger version of your chip swing—more arm swing, more wrist hinge and more body turn. The differences are pretty easy to spot, but what you might not recognize so easily is the footwork involved with both swings, which has a lot to do with how you shift your weight.

When you hit pitches and chips, you shift your weight to your left foot on your downswing, just like you do when you hit full shots from the fairway. Because your pitch swing is bigger than your chip swing (sometimes much bigger when you're pitching from long distance), you need a more pronounced shift. Focusing on your right ankle makes this happen almost automatically.

Rolling your right ankle and lifting your right heel through impact makes it easy to correctly shift your weight forward and turn through the shot.

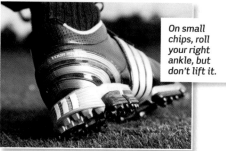

On small chips, roll your right ankle, but don't lift it.

HOW TO ROLL, LIFT AND SHIFT

Once you complete your pitch backswing, allow your right ankle to roll toward the target and your heel to rise slightly off the ground. This subtle bit of downswing footwork makes it easy to shift your weight forward and contact the ball with the majority of your weight on your left foot, allowing you to catch the ball crisp. This technique also works for your chip swing. The only difference is that your ankle only rolls—it doesn't lift—when you're hitting a chip.

TRY THIS!

MAKE YOUR PITCHES BITE
Accelerate then stop to get the check, please

If your pitch shots fly straight, but they land on the green without any spin and run past the hole, use the keys below to help your pitches land on your target and then grab the green harder than a miner's handshake.

STEP 1
On your backswing, point your thumbs at the sky and the butt of the club at the ground.

STEP 2
Come down sharply into the ball to get it rolling up the clubface.

STEP 3
Once you feel impact, stop your hands abruptly at waist height and keep them and your club low.

The faster you accelerate then stop, the more the ball will run up the face and grab in the grooves. That groove-grab adds spin.

61 | How to Lob It Close and Tight

"I can't lob the ball high, short and soft to save my life. How do the pros make this shot look so easy?"

"Don't copy the pro technique. This way is much easier: Make an early release."

EDEN FOSTER
Maidstone Club
East Hampton, N.Y.

CHECKPOINT

THE MISTAKE YOU SHOULD MAKE

On most shots, wristy impact is a recipe for disaster. However, when you have to pop the ball high and soft, you actually want to flip your wrists.

HOW TO COMMIT IT

Set up with a slightly open stance with your lob wedge and play the ball slightly back of center. Take your regular pitch backswing, but as you come back down, slow your arms and hips (something you do anyway if you often muff pitch shots) and quickly break your wrists through impact. Don't allow your arms to pass your body. If it helps to think of folding your left wrist or bowing your right, do it. While this is the opposite of traditional short-game advice, it's exactly what you need in this situation.

WHY IT WORKS

Flipping the club past your hands increases the effective loft of the clubface. So you get extra height on the shot that you normally wouldn't get if you adhered to the standard advice of keeping your hands ahead of the club at impact.

Flip the club past your hands to lob the ball high from rough.

HOW TO LOB WITH EASE

STEP 1
With your most lofted wedge, make your normal backswing and fully hinge your wrists.

STEP 2
As you approach impact, apply the brakes to your arms and step on the gas with your wrists.

STEP 3
Use your wrists to flip the clubhead under the ball and past your hands.

SWING THOUGHT

TRY THIS!

AIM FOR GROOVE 4
It's the key for lobbing from tight lies

Imagine contacting the ball between the third and fifth grooves up from the bottom of the clubface. This encourages you to make a descending blow, with the shaft leaning forward at impact. Your wrists won't break down, and the ball will climb up the face and into the air.

—Top 100 Teacher Charlie King

Trying to contact the ball between the thrid and fifth grooves gets you in the good habit of making a solid, descending strike.

Your scores drop
when your putts
do likewise.

If you miss your landing spot in the fairway by a few yards it's just a miss. Do the same on the green and that miss turns into a stroke lost forever. Yes, the demands of putting are severe, which is ironic since they involve the simplest motion. It boils down to that tiny target and the slips, slides, turns, breaks and bumps between it and where your ball lies. There's a lot to overcome, and a lot of questions to be answered. How fast will it go? How hard should I putt it? Is it downhill? Will it go straight or curve left?

There's a school of thought that says it takes years of experience to answer these questions correctly. The Top 100 Teachers disagree, and over the next several pages they will arm you with everything you need to putt the lights out from any distance. You know what the target is—here are the skills to find it.

6

HOLING OUT

It all comes down to the most perplexing part of
the game—putting. Here's how to get the ball
in the hole in far fewer strokes.

6

"I never think about my putting setup. I just step in and putt. Is this a mistake?"

"Use the following quick, two-part check to build a solid putting foundation every time."

TOM PATRI
Friar's Head
Riverhead, N.Y.

CHECK 1: FOREARMS

Your forearms should be level with each other at address. There are two ways to check this. If there's someone else on the putting green, have him stand behind you along the line of your putt at address and look at your forearms. Your right forearm should hide your left forearm. If you're alone, take your address position and look down at your forearms—if they're level with one another, you're good.

CHECK 2: EYES

At address, your eyes should be directly over your ball and your line of putt. This is crucial—even if your forearms are correct, if your eyes are too far outside the ball or too far inside the ball, a consistent path will be almost impossible.

EYES
Your eyes should be directly over your line of putt.

FOREARMS
Your forearms should be level with each other. From this angle, your right forearm correctly hides your left forearm.

BALL
Your ball should be positioned so that it's even with the left side of your chest.

WRONG! DON'T DO THIS

NO! Your arms are uneven and closed to the line of the putt.

NO! Your arms are uneven and open to the line of the putt.

NO! Your eyes are too far inside the line of putt.

NO! Your eyes are too far outside the line of the putt.

DRILL

TRY THIS!

GET YOUR PUTTS MOVING ON THE RIGHT TRACK

Use a CD to practice correctly setting your eyes over the ball

Fault: You consistently pull or push putts because your eyes are either too far inside the ball at address (causing a push) or too far outside the ball at address (causing a pull).

Fix: Position a ball in the little hole in the middle of an old music CD, shiny side up. Address the ball as if you were going to putt it and check where your eyes reflect on the CD. If your eyes are inside the ball, bend slightly forward from your hips until they move over the middle of the CD. If your eyes are outside the ball, bend slightly back from your hips. Positioning your eyes over the ball gives you the best view of the line and stops pull and push strokes in their tracks.

—*Top 100 Teacher Scott Sackett*

Use an old CD to see where your eyes sit at address. Eyes inside or outside the ball decrease the likelihood of hitting the putt on your intended line.

6

"I yip. I rush my stroke and often make a jabby move at the ball. How can I build better tempo and rhythm?"

"One thin dime can change you from a hitter to a stroker."

JIM SUTTIE
TwinEagle GC
Naples, Fla.
2000 Teacher of the Year

TECHNIQUE?

THE PROBLEM
You stab at the ball with your putter rather than making a smooth stroke, giving you zero speed control.

THE SOLUTION
Place a dime on the back of your putter as shown right and make your normal stroke. If you're stroking your putts using a pure pendulum motion, the dime will stay on the putter, no matter how far back and through you take the putter. If you're stabbing the ball, however, the dime will slide off the back of your club as soon as you transition from the backstroke to the forward stroke. You may not be able to tell if you're decelerating, but a dime will pick it up instantly.

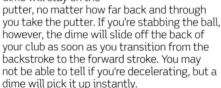

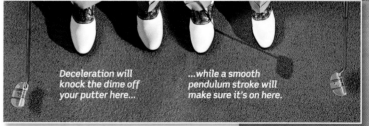

Deceleration will knock the dime off your putter here...

...while a smooth pendulum stroke will make sure it's on here.

DRILL

TRY THIS!

KEEP YOUR HEAD STILL

Your shadow will show you how to do it

One trait all good putters share is keeping their head still. You can't keep your putter on line if you move your head, nor can you keep your head still if you move the putter on the wrong path. A steady head allows your hands, arms and shoulders to move the putter correctly. On a sunny day, set up to the ball with your shadow directly in front of you. Place two balls on the green about a foot apart and address another one so that your head's shadow is between the two balls. Make your putting stroke, hold your finish and check your shadow to see if your head moved. If you have difficulty keeping your head still, use more arms and hands in your stroke with less shoulder movement.

—*Top 100 Teacher Paul Trittler*

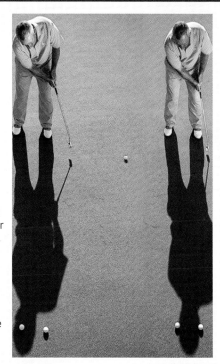

WRONG! If you move your head, your shadow knows.

RIGHT! Keep your head's shadow between the two balls.

6

"I either roll the ball too far or too long. What's wrong with my stroke?"

"The problem is probably in your grip. Here's how to find a good one and make distance control easy."

DAVID WRIGHT
Wright Balance Golf Academy, Arroyo Trabuco GC, Mission Viejo, Calif.

CHECKPOINT

TRY THIS!
The shortcut to saving strokes is in the palm of your hand. When you set the putter grip in the palm of your right hand, it gives you a stable, repeatable stroke that will do more for your game than beating balls on the driving range. Here's how to palm your way to better putting.

STEP 1: LET YOUR PALM BE THE PILOT
Set your putter behind the ball and position the grip in your right palm before placing your left hand on the club. The grip should be in line with your forearm [below, right], and the putter should feel like an extension of your arm. Avoid the fault of gripping the putter in your right fingers [above, right].

STEP 2: PUT THE PUSH ON
If your alignment is correct, your right palm will face the target, which is where you want it at impact. Your through-stroke should feel like you're pushing the ball down the target line with your right palm. This stroke will point the clubface at the hole and make it easier for you to release the putterhead for a more consistent end-over-end roll.

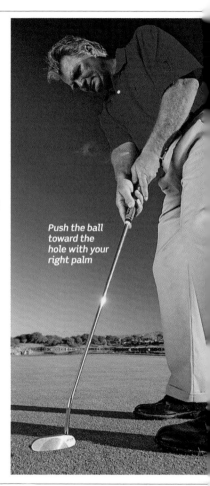

Push the ball toward the hole with your right palm

WRONG!

A finger hold makes it easy for your stroke to break down.

RIGHT!

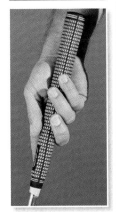

A palm grip gives you extra control.

DRILL

TRY THIS!

PUTT PIGEON-TOED

Take the tension out of short must-makes by toeing in your feet at address

One of the reasons why you miss more short putts than you should is that you move your head or lower body during your stroke. There are many reasons for this, the most important being that some short putts are real nerve-shakers because most short putts are to either save par or keep the damage to a minimum. Of course, your stroke may be to blame, but here's a way you can remove excess movement so you can make a solid stroke.

Take your normal putting address, then turn each toe in toward the middle of your stance, like you're pigeon-toed. Standing like this effectively restricts excess movement by eliminating the flexibility in your lower body. If you think you're too cool to putt pigeon-toed, then take it up with Arnold Palmer, who used this method frequently to help him remain steady over must-sink putts.

—*Top 100 Teacher Kellie Stenzel*

6

"I can read slope, but I never know how much it will affect the roll. How can I get good at green reading quickly?"

"Try this new green-reading trick: Finding the spine."

Golden Bear GC at Keene's Pointe Windermere, Fla.

STRATEGY

CHECK THIS!

You've probably heard TV announcers refer to the "fall line" when talking about a certain putt. What they're referring to is the road map to a particular hole position. The "spine" or fall line influences nearly every putt. Think of it as the Rosetta Stone to figuring out your line, a roadmap developed by Aim Point Technology. Once you identify it, you're on your way to fully understanding the putt you face.

A RIVER RUNS THROUGH IT
The are a multiple spines to every green (as indicated by the blue lines here), but only one spine per hole location. The spine runs through the hole.

SHARP CURVES
The farther the ball is from the spine, the more it will break. Maximum break occurs when you're putting at 90 degrees to the spine, and at the farthest point away from the spine. Putting downhill will also increase the amount of break.

THE SPINE LINE
The green doesn't have just one. Each hole position does.

THE BREAK LINE
Your ball's position in relation to the spine determines the big breaks

LEFT TO RIGHT
Putting uphill, any ball to the left of the spine will break from left to right. The closer the ball is to the spine, the straighter the putt.

RIGHT TO LEFT
A ball right of the spine will break from right to left.

WATCH WHERE THE WATER GOES

Every green has built-in drainage points. Knowing where they are is the key to finding the spine. Determine the highest point above the hole and walk to that spot. Imagine you have a hose and you're streaming water in the direction of the hole. The water will funnel toward the hole and follow a line as it drains off the green. That line is the spine.

BE YOUR OWN STIMPMETER

Find a flat spot on the practice green of your home course, take a stance that's about 12 inches wide and position the ball just inside your left heel. Swing your putter back so it goes directly in front of the big toe on your right foot. Hit five putts this way and note how far the ball rolls. Do the same thing when you're playing a different course. If the stroke that produces an eight-foot roll on your home course produces a 12-foot roll on the unfamiliar one, you'll know the greens are that much faster and that you should plan on more break.

—*Top 100 Teacher Fred Griffin*

TRY THIS!

READ GREENS LIKE A CADDIE

Six things the experts look for when judging slope

1 The faster the putting surface, the more break you have to allow for. This is because you'll be hitting the ball much softer and it will take more time to reach the hole. The more uphill it is, the less it will break because a firmer putt takes less time to reach the hole.

2 If the grass looks shiny along the line of your putt and darker when you look at the ball from behind the hole, you're putting down grain (that is, the grass is bending toward the sun). Expect a quicker putt and more break.

3 If the grass looks dark along the line of your putt, but shiny from behind the hole, you're putting against the grain. The putt will be slower and break less.

4 Feel the ground with your feet as you walk on the putting surface. Does the green feel firm (faster) or spongy (slower)? Do your leg muscles feel as if they are walking uphill toward the hole (slower) or downhill (faster)?

5 Watch the ball of everyone who putts before you. You'll get a sense what the ball will do near the hole and where it's most sensitive to break. Also note what any ball does when it goes beyond the hole. This gives you the perfect read and speed for any comeback.

6 Make your first read from behind the ball, looking toward the hole. Crouch down as low as you can to get a better view of the contours. Also, take note of water and drainage areas (putts often break toward these features), or mountains (putts break away from hills). If you're still unsure about your read, walk behind the hole to get a different perspective.

6

"I like my putter, but how do I know it's right for me?"

"You'll know you've picked the right putter when it matches your stroke. Here's how to do the research."

MIKE ADAMS
Hamilton Farms GC
Gladstone, N.J.

FUNDAMENTAL

THE MYTH
Depending on your preference, swing your putter straight-back-and-through or on a slight arc.

THE TRUTH
The design of your putter— not your preferred putting style—determines the type of path you should trace. Toe-weighted putters are engineered to open and close during your stroke and travel on an arc, and face-balanced models (ones that feature a centered shaft connection or a double-bend shaft) are engineered to remain square and travel on a straight line.

WHAT TO DO
Match your stroke to your putter, or buy a model that's designed to complement your putting style.

IF YOUR PUTTER IS FACE-BALANCED... Take it back and through on a straight line keeping the face square all the way.

Allow your arms to hang directly underneath your shoulders.

Bend from your hips more to get your eyes over the target line.

Play the ball slightly forward of center with the putterhead directly below your nose.

FACE-BALANCED STROKE
Move the putter straight back and through by rocking your shoulders like a teeter-totter. To ingrain the feel, place a club across your chest as shown. Hit some putts by pointing the triangle formed by the club and your arms away from the target and then to the target.

IF YOUR PUTTER IS TOE-WEIGHTED... Take it away to the inside of your target line, return it square and finish back on the inside.

Stand erect, with your eyes inside the target line.

Play the ball off your left armpit.

Position your hands in front of your shoulder line.

TOE-WEIGHTED STROKE
Since your hands are outside your arms, you'll naturally move the putter to the inside. The key is to maintain a free-flowing motion so you don't disturb the arc. Practice putting with your left arm only to develop a free motion. Think of how a gate swings open and shut.

CHECK THIS!

CHOOSE THE RIGHT TYPE OF HOSEL
Make sure it benefits your setup and stroke

1 If you push putts, try a **center-shafted putter** (such as the straight-in), which give you more direct control of the face position through impact.

2 If you're more of a "Crenshaw" putter, and like to gently roll the putter on an "inside-to-square-to-inside" stroke, you'll be better off with a **hosel/shaft attachment that favors the heel.**

3 If you pull more putts than you push, you'll fare better with a shaft/hosel-in-the-heel design (such as the **flare-tip**), which will hold off face rotation.

4 If your stroke is of the "straight-back-and-straight through" variety, you'll putt more consistently with a face-balanced putter, or one with a **shaft/hosel attachment closer to the center** of the head. Most face-balanced putters come with a double-bend shaft, so keep your eyes out for those.

5 If you strive to keep your hands ahead of the putter at impact, which many good putters do, a hosel/shaft offset like a **plumber-neck** will benefit your stroke. Plumber-neck hosels increase your ability to see how your putter is aligned at address. But they also impact your hand position.

6

Q

"My putts never start on the line I intended. Is it my face position or my stroke?"

A

"It's likely a combination of both. Try this five-step plan to get your putts tracking from the start."

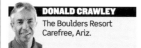

DONALD CRAWLEY
The Boulders Resort
Carefree, Ariz.

DRILL

HOW TO STAY ON YOUR LINE

It's critical to build a setup that gives you the best chance to get your ball rolling in the right direction, because a ball that starts off line stays off line. Here's a five-step plan to correctly position your body and putter on the line you've chosen.

STEP 2: ALIGN YOUR BALL

Draw a straight line across the logo on your ball. Use this mark to align your ball along the intended line of the putt by placing it underneath and parallel to the static line. Now you have a reference point to get your putterface pointed in the right direction.

STEP 1: FIND YOUR LINE

On the practice green, stand behind your ball and imagine how it will roll. Run a raised string along the starting point of the line and burn the image of what your starting line looks like into your brain. This physical representation of your putt line will give you an idea of what a straight line actually looks like.

STEP 3: AIM YOUR PUTTER

Remove the string and sole your putterhead on the ground. Align the face so that the top edge makes a perpendicular angle with the mark on your ball. This will ensure that your putter starts the ball on the correct line after contact, as long as you don't dramatically open or close the face.

STEP 4: SET YOUR EYES

Set your eyes over the ball and parallel to your intended line. If you set your eyes to the inside of the ball your stroke will have a tendency to move inside and push your putts; set your eyes outside and you'll likely pull your putts. Either way, you'll miss the putt.

STEP 5: ALIGN YOUR BODY

Allow your arms to hang straight down from your shoulders, and then place your hands on the grip. Loose, free-hanging arms are needed to create the tension-free stroke that you need to be a consistent putter.

TRY THIS!

HOW TO ROLL WITH PERFECT SPEED
This drill will give you the right pace for short putts

Secure a scorecard pencil between two sets of tees in front of the hole as shown at right. Putt a few balls from anywhere from three to five feet from the hole. The idea is to hit these putts with enough force that the ball pops over the pencil and then into the hole. You'll quickly learn that to sink your putts with the proper amount of speed; you can't baby the ball to the hole, nor can you rocket it because too much speed will pop the ball over both the pencil and the hole.

Once you get to the point where you can consistently pop eight out of 10 putts over the pencil and into the hole, remove the pencil and try to sink your putts with the same velocity through the two tees— these putts should always hit somewhere on the back of the cup. Then remove the tees and work on maintaining the same speed and line.

—Top 100 Teacher Dr. Gary Wiren

The speed that will pop the ball over a pencil and into the cup is perfect for short putts.

6

"I have no idea if what I'm doing is correct. What should I do?"

"You need a new outlook on your green game. Try this new method that's been proven to make putting easy."

ERIC ALPENFELS
Pinehurst Golf Academy
Pinehurst Resort
Pinehurst, N.C.

STRATEGY

THE NEW THEORY

You should look at the hole—not the ball—from the moment you set the club behind the ball until you complete your putting stroke.

WHO TOOK PART

Forty players ranging in handicap from eight to 36. They were divided into two 20-person groups, with each group balanced in terms of handicap, age and gender. One was the experimental group. The other was the control group. This control group used the conventional method of looking at the ball while putting throughout the test.

THE EXPERIMENT

Using the conventional method of looking at the ball, both groups putted nine balls to holes ranging from three feet to 43 feet away. The results were statistically equal. Next, the control group putted one ball to each of nine targets in random order. The experimental group did the same but with one huge change: They were instructed to go through their normal pre-putt routine, but rather than looking at the ball as they made their stroke, they were told to look at the hole. Then we compared the two groups. The results will surprise you.

THE SHOCKING RESULTS!

1. Long putts end up significantly closer to the hole when you look at the hole while making your stroke. On average, after all was said and done, on putts between 28 feet and 43 feet in length, the experimental group (those who looked at the hole) had slightly less than 28 inches remaining.

By comparison, on the same 28- to 43-foot-long putts, the control group (those who looked at the ball) left themselves nearly 37 inches to the hole. That means the experimental group was 24 percent closer. Those nine inches could be the difference between a two-putt and a three-putt.

2. Looking at the hole may be more effective on short putts, too. On putts between three feet and eight feet, the experimental group left an average of just under nine inches to the hole. On the same putts, the control group ended up with leaves that averaged 12.5 inches. Strictly speaking, that's not statistically significant, but those inches might be the difference between a routine tap-in and the occasional short miss.

Subjects were told to look at the hole the entire time.

THE NEW WAY TO PUTT

1 Address the ball and place your putter behind it.

2 Start looking at the hole, and don't look back at the ball. (We promise it's still there.)

3 Hit your putt, and keep looking at the hole until you complete your stroke.

RESULTS: LOOKING AT THE HOLE

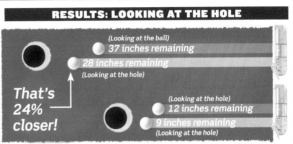

(Looking at the ball)
37 inches remaining

28 inches remaining
(Looking at the hole)

That's 24% closer!

(Looking at the hole)
12 inches remaining

9 inches remaining
(Looking at the hole)

Any golfer who's had an important putt burn the lip of the hole knows every inch is precious on the green. This graph clearly shows that looking at the hole, not the ball, will pay off dramatically.

WHY IT WORKS

There are three main reasons why the new method improves on your old one:

1 You're using both eyes to to see your target, giving you highly accurate depth perception.

2 Maybe it was a fear of whiffing the putt, but testers who looked at the hole maintained their posture like statues.

3 Testers who looked at the hole didn't decelerate through the ball. In other words, they established natural speed control.

MORE RESULTS

Two other facts of note from our research: From 13 to 23 feet, both methods produced similar results. Neither method produced more holed putts from any distance.

6

You're going to find trouble every time you play. The trick isn't avoiding it—it's learning to get out of it.

Face facts: Bad shots happen, and even good ones end up in trouble because of bad bounces, strange kicks and other "rub of the green" effects that defy explanation but nonetheless are a very real part of the game.

A trouble situation is any one that prohibits you from making your regular swing. Most often it takes the form of an obstacle between you and your target. Other times it's the lie itself, like when your ball comes to rest in ankle-deep rough or a nasty greenside bunker.

Point is, finding trouble is something every golfer does. The trick is getting out of it. In this section the Top 100 Teachers describe how to overcome the most common of the literally dozens of forms of trouble you can find on the course. Learn and perfect these escapes and you'll be sitting pretty—even when your ball isn't.

7

GETTING OUT OF TROUBLE

Even the best-made plans sometimes
go haywire. Here's how to get out of any nasty
predicament on the course.

7

"Bunkers—I'm not very good at getting out of them. What's the secret everone but me seems to know?"

"No secrets, just a few basics that make escaping bunkers easier than it looks."

SCOTT SACKETT
McCormick Ranch GC
Scottsdale, Ariz.

FUNDAMENTAL

DO THIS!
Follow these three easy steps for foolproof escapes from normal lies.

STEP 1
With the flagstick representing 12:00 on a clock face, open up your stance just slightly, so your feet, hips and shoulders are pointing to 11:30. Aim the leading edge of your sand wedge at the flag.

12.00

Learning bunker basics makes any sandy lie easy.

STEP 2

Spread your feet two inches wider than normal. A wider stance helps quiet your legs so you can correctly swing more with your arms. Plus, a wider stance makes it easier to repeat your swing and control your clubhead.

Keep your legs wide and quiet.

STEP 3

These adjustments will help you attack the ball from the inside with the clubface square to the target, so not only will you get out of the bunker, the ball will fly at your target.

Attack from the inside.

TRY THIS!

PUT YOUR DIVOT IN THE RIGHT PLACE

This simple drill tells you a lot about the quality of your bunker swing

A perfect bunker swing enters the sand about two to three inches behind the ball, skims a half-inch to an inch under the surface, then emerges about three inches in front of where the ball rested. The clubhead never touches the ball itself. The sand carries the ball out.

To see if you're doing it correctly, draw parallel lines in the sand about six inches apart, drop a ball between them and make your swing. Check the guide at right to see if you're entering the sand too early, entering the sand too late or taking too large of a divot.

—Top 100 Teacher Paul Marchand

Perfect. The club never touched the ball.

Too deep. This one was left in the bunker.

Entered too early. Left it in the bunker again.

Entered too late. This one was bladed over the green.

7

"My sand shots run out too far. How do I make the ball hit and stop from a bunker?"

"The trick is in your setup and how you align your shoulders at address."

TODD SONES
Impact Golf Schools
White Deer Run GC
Vernon Hills, Ill.

TECHNIQUE

THE SITUATION
You have a good lie in a greenside bunker, but you've short-sided yourself and have just a few paces of green between you and the flag.

THE SOLUTION
You need a high, soft sand shot that stops on a dime. Here are four easy steps to make it sit.

Use your most-lofted wedge and a lot of wrist action to hit the ball high from short distance.

HOW TO MAKE SAND SHOTS BITE

STEP 1
Select your most-lofted wedge. Position the ball slightly forward in your stance and move the handle of the club in-line with your right thigh to add extra loft to the clubface.

STEP 2
Spread your stance by taking a step out with your right foot and dig both feet into the sand a half-inch for balance. Your shaft should now point just left of the center of your torso.

STEP 3
Make sure your shoulder and shaft lines form an angled "T." Your job is to recreate the "T" at impact so that your club enters the sand with the same amount of loft it had at address. Swing your club more with your arms and wrists, using minimum shoulder movement.

STEP 4
Keep your chest pointed down and swing your arms and hands underneath your body. Move onto your left hip through impact to keep the club from releasing past your hands. Try to keep your hands and clubhead low in your follow-through so the clubface stays open.

7

Q

I'm okay when the ball is sitting up, but almost always leave it in the bunker when it's buried. Please help!"

A

"For nasty buried lies, your best bet is to go pound sand!"

EDEN FOSTER
Maidstone Club
East Hampton, N.Y.

TECHNIQUE

THE SITUATION

Your ball is three-quarters buried in loose sand toward the upper part of a steep lip. Even taking a stance won't be easy. You'll have no trouble swinging the club back, but deep sand and the overhanging lip will severely limit your follow-through.

THE SOLUTION

Realistically, you can't do much more to the ball than dislodge it. But guess what? That's about all you have to do! In fact, you're free to commit the most common bunker error of all time and quit on the shot. More good news? You get to make a violent, no-finish swing and pound that stupid bunker!

Be sure to keep most of your weight on your left side.

Anchor your back foot by digging it deeper into the sand than your front foot.

There's no need to turn your right arm over your left after impact because any follow-through will be minimal.

Your clubhead should literally burrow into the sand beneath the ball.

The ball can plug, but it can't hide.

HOW TO DO IT

STEP 1
Use whichever of your wedges has the most bounce and open the blade just a bit at address. As you finish settling into your posture, dig your back foot deeper in the sand than your front.

STEP 2
Make a full backswing, then slam the club powerfully into the sand an inch or two behind your ball as if you're trying to bury the clubhead.

STEP 3
Don't expect any follow-through, just a soft rebound effect as your club emerges lazily from the sand. Meanwhile your ball and a half-cup of sand are already crossing the bunker lip on their way to the green.

WHY IT WORKS
The difference between this shot and one where you quit on it unintentionally is that, in this instance, you are accelerating the clubhead, not decelerating it. As a result, you can still displace enough sand to get the ball up and out of the bunker on an almost vertical trajectory.

TRY THIS!

BEAT NASTY BUNKERS
Here you need to carve it out more than blast it out
You've heard that you should "float" the ball out on a cushion of sand, but whoever said that has never been to your local muni, where the bunkers look more like wet concrete. Your normal bunker shot won't work here. You'll need to square the clubface and dig it out.
—*Top 100 Teacher Brady Riggs*

1: SET UP LEFT
Lean your weight on your left side to create a digging angle of attack, and set the face square.

2: DIG IT OUT
Hit just behind the ball and drive the leading edge into the sand.

3: FINISH LOW
You're not trying to splash sand here, just to get the lead edge deep enough to pop the ball out.

7

"Once I'm in the trees I usually stay there. I can't keep the ball under the branches. Any advice?"

"Never use more than a 6-iron, then make the following changes to dial in the distance you need."

DR. GARY WIREN
Trump International
West Palm Beach, Fla.
1987 Teacher of the Year

TECHNIQUE

This only works if you swing to a full finish. The ball will fly low enough to avoid the trouble and travel far enough to hit the green.

THE SITUATION
You've missed the fairway, and though you're only 100 yards from the green, a low-hanging branch prevents you from playing a wedge.

THE STRATEGY
Step 1: Stay aggressive—never let a tree or its limbs come between you and a chance for birdie.
Step 2: Determine which is the highest-lofted club in your bag that will keep the ball under the branch.

Step 3: Mix and match your grip (how much you choke down on the handle) and backswing length to produce the appropriate distance.

HOW TO DO IT
For the shot depicted here, a 6-iron is the highest loft that will keep the ball under the limb. Let's say you normally hit a 6-iron 160 yards. Here's the trick to hitting it to whatever yardage you need.

160 yds
Take your normal grip on the end of the handle.

150 yds
Now choke down to the middle of the grip. This takes ten yards off the shot.

140 yds
If you choke all the way down to the bottom, that subtracts ten more yards.

140 yds
With a full swing you'll still produce 140 yards.

120 yds
Shorten your backswing by 10 inches (hands chest high) to hit it 20 yards less.

100 yds
Shorten your backswing another 10 inches (hands at hip height) to take off another 20 yards.

OPTION-MINDED

Mixing and matching the three choke distances with the three different backswing lengths allows you to produce seven distances with each one of your irons.

SHOTMAKING

TRY THIS!

MAKE A BACK-HANDED ESCAPE

Flip the club when you can't take a normal stance

STEP 1
Turn your back to the target, stand about a half-foot to the right of the ball and grip your wedge in the middle of the handle. Flip your club around so that the face points at your target with the club resting on its toe.

STEP 2
Cock your club up by bending your right elbow (keep your upper arm still). Add just a touch of wrist hinge.

STEP 3
Straighten your arm and slap your clubhead into the back of the ball.

This is is a trick shot that's actually very easy to pull off with a little practice. Make sure you accelerate all the way to the ball so the club doesn't flip past your hands and hit the ball thin.

—Top 100 Teacher Tom Stickney

7

"There are some big trees at my course. How can I hit a solid shot when I'm caught behind one?"

"Make an aggressive move and then recoil at impact to bust the ball (and not your club)."

ANNE CAIN
Anne Cain Golf Academy
Amelia Island, Fla.

THE SITUATION
You're in one of those curse-causing situations when the ball comes to rest at the base of a tree or other obstacle from which you cannot take relief without taking a penalty. You can make a full backswing, but you can't follow through without slamming the club into the trunk or the impediment.

THE SOLUTION
Most golfers try to swing slow here, but that leads to mis-hits (usually in the form of fat contact with the ball dribbling only a few yards forward). Keep your speed the same, but make a smaller swing so you can pull the club back at impact.

DANGER! Clubs can—and will—break after striking large objects. If you have any doubts, take a drop or play a short chip shot.

WRIST AT TARGET
Since you're only making a little half swing with zero follow-through, make sure the back of your left hand points where you want the ball to go as you strike it.

BURY IT
If you're not comfortable pulling the club back, then simply bury the club in the dirt at impact and leave it there, like you're blasting from a buried bunker lie.

STEEP CONTACT
Come down sharply on the ball, like you're trying to pound it into the ground, and make sure that all of your weight is over your left foot at impact or you'll catch the shot fat.

HOW TO PUNCH A RESTRICTED SWING

STEP 1

Select one of your mid- or short irons (a shorter club is easier to control because it doesn't travel as fast), take a shoulder-width stance and play the ball as close to the middle as possible.

Play the ball as close to the middle of your stance as possible.

STEP 2

Take your club back by hinging your wrists quickly and fully so that the clubhead gets above your hands almost immediately. Swing your hands back only to hip height (your goal is to advance the ball from this lie, not hole it out).

Set the club higher than your hands in your half-backswing.

STEP 3

Swing your arms sharply down on the ball, as if you're trying to take a deep divot. Keep your speed up or you'll risk hitting the shot fat. As soon as you make contact, pull the club away from the target. Make the club recoil like it just hit a tire. That'll stop you from striking the trunk while still getting plenty of juice on the ball.

7

74 | How to Use Half a Swing

"What can you do when you can't make a backswing— foot-wedge the ball out?"

"This is a toughie, but it can be done. The trick is to generate speed in a short amount of space."

SHAWN HUMPHRIES
Cowboys Golf Club
Grapevine, Tex.

TECHNIQUE

THE SITUATION
Your ball is up against a tree or other obstacle which prevents you from making a complete backswing.

THE SOLUTION
Don't go from worse to worst. Look at what you can reasonably accomplish and avoid a double penalty. In most situations like this your only play is a less-than-full punch swing. Follow the steps at right to catch the ball as cleanly as possible and get it back in play.

GET GROUNDED
The mistake here is rushin your transition. Your goal to simply brush the groun underneath the ball. Do that and the shot will take care of itself.

GET PREPPED
Make at least 10 practice swings. With each rehearsal, feel how far you can take the club back and concentrate on making as smooth a transition as possible.

HOW TO ESCAPE WITH ONLY A HALF SWING

STEP 1
Plan a safe route
See what's possible. Likely, there won't be much. In most instances your goal should be to get the ball back in the fairway.

STEP 2
Get set
Make sure you select the correct club with enough loft to get you over any obstacles or rough. The longest club you should use is a 7-iron. Set up square to where you want the ball to land with a narrower stance than normal.

STEP 3
Rehearse a half-swing
Choke down and make several practice swings. A Tour player will make 10 to 15 practice strokes when hitting an unfamiliar shot like this. Make enough practice strokes so that you know that you won't hit the tree [photos, right] and you can brush the ground.

STEP 4
Build some trust
At the end of your practice strokes, get comfortable in your setup, flex your knees and commit to the shot. Focus on making solid contact and a full follow-through. You've hit punch shots thousands of times—this one is no different.

Make several practice swings to find out how far back you can take your club.

This is an all-arms shot that needs a soft transition from backswing to downswing.

DRILL

TRY THIS!

TRAPPED UNDER A TREE? USE YOUR PUTTER!
Pop down on the ball and watch it run

You may not think much about your putter until you reach the green, but the flatstick can be a tremendously versatile trouble club elsewhere on the course.

The next time you find yourself in a spot where it's hard to get an iron on the ball and hit it out to the fairway or on the green, try this. Position the ball roughly 12 inches to the right of your right foot. Swing your putter back with a lot of wrist action and then pop the putterhead down hard on the back of the ball. The ball will shoot out low with a lot of topspin, which will allow it to cover a lot of distance without much effort.

Bring the putter down hard on the back of the ball.

7

I struggle to advance the ball from deep grass. How can I get this one to fly straight?"

"Replace your swing with a gouging move that, while lacking beauty, gets you back into the hole."

STEVE BOSDOSH
The Members Club at
Four Streams
Beallsville, Md.

THE SITUATION

Your ball has come to rest in the rough. The grass isn't long but it's thick, covering the ball on all sides.

THE SOLUTION

Throw any chances of hitting the green from this lie out the window. This is gouge time—a 9-iron at best. You're going to use a lot of the elements from your bunker swing, but instead of sliding your club through sand, you'll slam it steeply into the back of the ball and do it fast enough so the grass doesn't grab the hosel and pull the ball left and into possibly deeper trouble.

TIGHTEN UP
Thick rough will yank the clubface left through impact. If your normal grip pressure is a "7," make your grip here a solid "10."

HOW TO GOUGE IT FROM THE JUNK

CLUB OPTIONS
If you can see the top half of your ball, use your 9-iron (stronger players can use an 8-iron). If only a small circle on the top of the ball is visible, opt for your sand wedge.

GET CLOSER
Stand closer to the ball. This makes your club more upright, helping you to hit down on the ball and minimize turf contact.

HIT AND QUIT
The rough likely will stop your swing just after impact. Focus on what's happening before you strike the ball, not after.

STEP 1
Stand closer to the ball and choke up a few inches on the handle. Notice how this makes your shaft more upright (a good thing in this situation). Aim slightly right of where you want the ball to land.

Grip the club tightly.

STEP 2
Play the ball back and increase your grip pressure. If you don't have a firm hold on the club the grass will turn it over and the ball will go left. Forward-press your hands so the shaft leans toward the target.

Play the ball back.

STEP 3
Hinge the club back quickly. On normal swings you start hinging your wrists when your hands reach hip height. Here, you want fully cocked wrists by the time your hands reach thigh height.

Start your swing by hinging your wrists.

STEP 4
From the top, swing down sharply and with plenty of force. Feel like you're pulling the handle of the club down into the ball. Keep your legs quiet (notice how little they move in Steps 3 and 4).

Pull the handle of the club down to the ball.

7

The Top 100 Teachers In America

The nation's most exclusive—and talented—team of teaching experts

Mike Adams
Hamilton Farms Golf Club
Gladstone, N.J.

Rob Akins
Spring Creek Ranch
Collierville, Tenn.

Eric Alpenfels
Pinehurst Golf Academy
Pinehurst Resort
Pinehurst, N.C.

Todd Anderson
Sea Island Golf
Learning Center
St. Simons Island, Ga.

Robert Baker
Logical Golf
Miami Beach, Fla.

Jimmy Ballard (Emeritus)
Ballard Swing Connection
Key Largo, Fla.

Rick Barry
Sea Pines Resort
Hilton Head Island, S.C.

Peggy Kirk Bell (Emeritus)
Pine Needles Resort
Southern Pines, N.C.

Mike Bender
Timacuan Golf Club
Lake Mary, Fla.

Steve Bosdosh
Members Club at
Four Streams
Beallsville, Md.

Michael Breed
Sunningdale Country Club
Scarsdale, N.Y.

Brad Brewer
Brad Brewer Golf Academy
Shingle Creek Resort
Orlando, Fla.

Anne Cain
Anne Cain Golf Academy
The Golf Club of
Amelia Island
Amelia Island, Fla.

Jason Carbone
Baltusrol Golf Club
Springfield, N.J.

Chuck Cook (Emeritus)
Chuck Cook Golf Academy
Austin, Tex.

Donald Crawley
The Boulders Golf Academy
Carefree, Ariz.

John Dahl
Oxbow Country Club
Oxbow, N.D.

Bill Davis
Jupiter Hills Club
Tequesta, Fla.

Mike Davis
Walters Golf Academy
Las Vegas, Nev.

Manuel De La Torre
(Emeritus)
Milwaukee Country Club
River Hills, Wisc.

Glenn Deck
Pelican Hill Golf Academy
The Resort at Pelican Hill
Newport Coast, Calif.

Dom DiJulia
Dom DiJulia School of Golf
Jericho National Golf Club
New Hope, Pa.

John Elliott Jr.
Golden Ocala Golf and
Equestrian Club
Ocala, Fla.

Chuck Evans
Medicus Golf Institute
Destin, Fla.

Jim Flick (Emeritus)
Taylor Made Performance
and Research Lab
Carlsbad, Calif.

Bill Forrest
Troon Country Club
Scottsdale, Ariz.

Eden Foster
Maidstone Club
East Hampton, N.Y.

Jane Frost
Jane Frost Golf School
Sandwich, Mass.

Bryan Gathright
Oak Hills Country Club
San Antonio, Tex.

David Glenz
David Glenz Golf Academy
Crystal Springs Resort
Franklin, N.J.

Patrick Goss
Northwestern University
Evanston, Ill.

Rick Grayson
Rivercat Golf Club
Springfield, Mo.

Fred Griffin
Grand Cypress
Academy of Golf
Orlando, Fla.

Ron Gring
Gring Golf
Timber Creek Golf Club
Daphne, Ala.

Roger Gunn
Tierra Rejada Golf Club
Moorpark, Calif.

Mark Hackett
Old Palm Golf Club
Palm Beach Gardens, Fla.

Martin Hall
Ibis Golf & Country Club
West Palm Beach, Fla.

Hank Haney
Hank Haney Golf
McKinney, Tex.

Jim Hardy
Jim Hardy Golf
Houston, Tex.

Craig Harmon
Oak Hill Country Club
Rochester, N.Y.

Butch Harmon Jr.
Butch Harmon
School of Golf
Henderson, Nev.

Michael Hebron
(Emeritus)
Smithtown Landing
Golf Club
Smithtown, N.Y.

Shawn Humphries
Cowboys Golf Club
Grapevine, Tex.

Don Hurter
Castle Pines Golf Club
Castle Rock, Colo.

Ed Ibarguen
Duke University Golf Club
Durham, N.C.

Hank Johnson
Greystone Golf Club
Birmingham, Ala.

Charlie King
Reynolds Golf Academy
Reynolds Golf Plantation
Greensboro, Ga.

Jerry King
Kapalua Golf Academy
Lahaina, Maui, Hawaii

Peter Kostis
Kostis/McCord
Learning Center
Grayhawk Golf Club
Scottsdale, Ariz.

Don Kotnik
Toledo Country Club
Toledo, Ohio

Peter Krause
Hank Haney International
Junior Golf Academy
Hilton Head, S.C.

Mike LaBauve
Westin Kierland Resort
Scottsdale, Ariz.

Sandy LaBauve
Westin Kierland Resort
Scottsdale, Ariz.

David Leadbetter
(Emeritus)
David Leadbetter
Golf Academy
Champions Gate, Fla.

Rod Lidenberg
Prestwick Golf Club
Woodbury, Minn.

Michael Lopuszynski
David Glenz Golf Academy
Crystal Springs Resort
Franklin, N.J.

Jack Lumpkin
Sea Island Golf
Learning Center
St. Simons Island, Ga.

Keith Lyford
Golf Academy at
Old Greenwood
Truckee, Calif.

Bill Madonna
Bill Madonna Golf Academy
Orlando, Fla.

Tim Mahoney
Talking Stick Golf Club
Scottsdale, Ariz.

Mike Malaska
Superstition Mountain
Superstition Mountain, Ariz.

Paul Marchand
Shadowhawk Golf Club
Richmond, Tex.

Lynn Marriott
Vision 54
Phoenix, Ariz.

Rick Martino
Motion Golf
Palm Beach Gardens, Fla.

Rick McCord
McCord Golf Academy
Orange Lake Country Club
Orlando, Fla.

Gerald McCullagh
University of Minnesota
Les Bolstad Golf Course
Falcon Heights, Minn.

Mike McGetrick
Colorado Golf Club
Parker, Colo.

Jim McLean (Emeritus)
Jim McLean Golf School
Miami, Fla.

Eddie Merrins (Emeritus)
Bel-Air Country Club
Los Angeles, Calif.

Brian Mogg
Brian Mogg
Performance Center
Golden Bear Golf Club at
Keene's Point
Windermere, Fla.

Bill Morelli
Academy of Golf Dynamics
Austin, Tex.

Jerry Mowlds
Pumpkin Ridge Golf Course
North Plains, Ore.

Scott Munroe
Adios Golf Club
Coconut Creek, Fla.

Jim Murphy
Jim Murphy Golf
Sugar Creek Country Club
Sugar Land, Tex.

Tom Ness
Reunion Golf Club
Hoschton, Ga.

Pia Nilsson
Vision 54
Phoenix, Ariz.

Dan Pasquariello
Pebble Beach Golf Academy
Pebble Beach, Calif.

Tom Patri
Friar's Head
Riverhead, N.Y.

Bruce Patterson
Butler National Golf Course
Oak Brook, Ill.

Dave Pelz (Emeritus)
Dave Pelz Golf
Spicewood, Tex.

Mike Perpich
RiverPines Golf
Alpharetta, Ga.

Gale Peterson
Sea Island Golf
Learning Center
St. Simons Island, Ga.

E.J. Pfister
Gaillardia Golf Club
Oklahoma City, Okla.

David Phillips
Titleist Performance
Institute
Oceanside, Calif.

Carol Preisinger
Kiawah Island Club
Johns Island, S.C.

Kip Puterbaugh
The Aviara Golf Academy
Carlsbad, Calif.

Nancy Quarcelino
Kings Creek Golf Club
Spring Hill, Tenn.

Carl Rabito
Rabito Golf
Bolingbrook G.C.
Bolingbrook, Ill.

Dana Rader
Dana Rader Golf School
Ballantyne Resort
Charlotte, N.C.

Brad Redding
The Resort Club at
Grande Dunes
Myrtle Beach, S.C.

Brady Riggs
Woodley Lakes Golf Course
Van Nuys, Calif.

Phil Ritson (Emeritus)
Orange County National
Golf Center
Orlando, Fla.

Phil Rodgers (Emeritus)
Carlton Oaks
Santee, Calif.

Scott Sackett
Scott Sackett Golf
McCormick Ranch Golf Club
Scottsdale, Ariz.

Adam Schriber
Crystal Mountain Resort
Thompsonville, Mich.

Craig Shankland
(Emeritus)
LPGA International
Daytona Beach, Fla.

Ted Sheftic
Bridges Golf Club
Abbottstown, Pa.

Laird Small
Pebble Beach Golf Academy
Pebble Beach, Calif.

Randy Smith
Royal Oaks Country Club
Dallas, Tex.

Rick Smith
Treetops Resort
Gaylord, Mich.

Todd Sones
Impact Golf Schools
White Deer Golf Club
Vernon Hills, Ill.

Mitchell Spearman
Manhattan Woods Golf Club
West Nyack, N.Y.

Kellie Stenzel
Atlantic Golf Club
Bridgehampton, N.Y.

Tom Stickney
The Club at Cordillera
Vail, Colo.

Dr. Jim Suttie (Emeritus)
The Club at TwinEagles
Naples, Fla.

Jon Tattersall
Terminus Club
Atlanta, Ga.

Dr. T.J. Tomasi
PGA Center for Golf Learning
and Performance
Port St. Lucie, Fla.

Bob Toski (Emeritus)
Toski-Battersby Golf
Learning Center
Coconut Creek, Fla.

Paul Trittler
Kostis/McCord
Learning Center
Grayhawk Golf Club
Scottsdale, Ariz.

J.D. Turner
The Turner Golf Group
Savannah, Ga.

Stan Utley
Grayhawk Learning Center
Scottsdale, Ariz.

Carl Welty
Jim McLean Golf Schools
LaQuinta, Calif.

Chuck Winstead
The University Club
Baton Rouge, La.

Dr. Gary Wiren (Emeritus)
Trump International
West Palm Beach, Fla.

Mark Wood
Cornerstone Club
Montrose, Colo.

Dr. David Wright
Wright Balance
Golf Academy
Arroyo Trabuco GC
Mission Viejo, CA

Get more information
on *GOLF Magazine's*
Top 100 Teachers and
the Top Teachers by
Region, plus exclusive
video tips and drills at
golf.com/instruction

LESSON FINDER
Choose your flaw
then read the story
that tells you how
to go fix it.

EXCLUSIVE VIDEOS
Personal lessons
from the game's
best teachers in
high-quality
streaming video.

**LIVE TOP 100
TEACHER'S BLOG**
Get swing advice—in
an instant—in our live
one-on-one chats with
the Top 100 Teachers
in America.

GOLF.com

Credits

Editor David M. Clarke
Creative Director Paul Crawford
Executive Editor Eamon Lynch
Art Director Paul Ewen
Managing Editors David DeNunzio (Instruction), Gary Perkinson (Production), Robert Sauerhaft (Equipment)
Editor at Large Connell Barrett
Deputy Managing Editor Michael Chwasky (Instruction & Equipment)
Senior Editors Alan Bastable, Joseph Passov (Travel/Course Rankings), Michael Walker Jr.
Deputy Art Director Karen Ha
Photo Editors Carrie Boretz (Associate), Jesse Reiter (Assistant)
Senior Writer Cameron Morfit
Assistant Editor Steven Beslow
Administrative Assistant Jessica Marksbury

Publisher Dick Raskopf
Associate Advertising Director Nathan Stamos
Director of Business Development Brad J. Felenstein
General Manager Peter Greer **VP & General Manager** (Golf.Com) Ken Fuchs
Business Development Manager Russ Vance
Human Resources Director Liz Mattila

Managing Editor, SI Golf Group James P. Herre

Editor, Sport Illustrated Group Terry McDonell
Executive Editor Michael Bevans
Managing Editor, SI.com Paul Fichtenbaum
V.P. Advertising Sales Jeff Griffing
Chief Marketing Officer Andrew R. Judelson
President, SI Digital Jeff Price
V.P. Consumer Marketing John Reese
V.P. Communications Scott Novak

NEWS GROUP
Executive V.P. John Squires
President & Group Publisher Mark Ford
Senior V.P. & Group General Manager John B. Reuter

Executive Editor Charlie Hanger
Executive Producer Christopher Shade **Deputy Editor** David Dusek
Producer Ryan Reiterman **Associate Art Director** Omar Sharif
Sr. Ad Operations Manager Elise LeScoezec

Publisher Richard Fraiman
General Manager Steven Sandonato
Executive Director, Marketing Services Carol Pittard
Director, Retail & Special Sales Tom Mifsud
Director, New Product Development Peter Harper
Assistant Director, Bookazine Marketing Laura Adam
Assistant Publishing Director, Brand Marketing Joy Butts
Associate Counsel Helen Wan
Brand & Licensing Manager Alexandra Bliss
Design & Prepress Manager Anne-Michelle Gallero
Book Production Manager Susan Chodakiewicz

WORDS
GOLF MAGAZINE'S
Top 100 Teachers
in America with
David DeNunzio

BOOK DESIGN
Paul Ewen

PHOTOGRAPHY
Angus Murray

SI IMAGING
Geoffrey A. Michaud
(Director),
Dan Larkin,
Robert M. Thompson

**ADDITIONAL
PHOTOGRAPHY**
Bob Atkins: 12-13, 24,
43 [L], 72-73, 74-75,
80, 81 [L], 83 [BR], 91,
92, 114-115, 137, 141
[BR], 147 [R], 148, 149
[L], 154, 155 [L], 157,
163 [BR]
Neil Beckerman: 55
D2 Productions:
29 [BR], 62, 98-99,
100-101, 104-105,
106-107, 112-113,
120-121, 122-123,
125 [R], 142, 145 [BR],
158, 173 [R]
Sam Greenwood:
39 [R], 65 [BR]
Leonard Kamsler:
32-33, 36-37, 89 [BR],
144, 145 [L]
Ian Logan: 52
Schecter Lee: 51 [BR],
54, 102-103, 108-109,
110-111, 116-117,
118-119, 130, 172,
173 [L]
Fred Vuich: 45 [BR], 48,
49 [L], 57 [BR], 81 [BR],
162, 163 [L]

ILLUSTRATIONS
Phil Franke: 153
Robin Griggs:
124-125, 150
Barry Ross: 171